FREE RANGE DOGS AND COCONUTS

Discovering a Dream Home in Sri Lanka

Angela Coe

ISBN
Paperback 979-8-89588-294-8
Hardcase 979-8-89744-552-3

Acknowledgements

First, I would like to point out how lucky I have been that my brother Hargreaves (Michael) so readily agreed to join me in moving out to Sri Lanka and sharing the life described in this book. The book would never have been written if my sister Jennie and many of my friends had not pestered me to write about my travels. I promised I would write books when I reached the age of eighty. By then, I thought I might prefer to relive my memories rather than travel. Having now turned 80, I am keeping my promise.

To have had the friendship of Sita and all her family has meant a lot, far more than told here. All the help we received from them made our lives so much easier and happier.

Bandusena, who not only worked for us but also taught us so much about all forms of life found in the garden, took it upon himself to cook wonderful curries from unfamiliar vegetables. He also showed us the way festivals were conducted in our new home. .

By the same author

Monkeying Around at Sea

For

My Brother Hargreves

With love

Contents

What though the spicy breezes,

Blow soft o'er Ceylon Isle,

Though every prospect pleases,

And only man is vile

Reginald Herber 1819-Rector of Hodnet

Chapter One

The Start

———— ❖ ————

"I just cannot believe it," I said, as we returned home from a visit to our local tip, fondly known by ourselves and fellow garbologists as the Emporium. An outing there was far more exciting than going to the high street shops. People throw out the most amazing stuff these days. We have found boxes of envelopes all stamped, a pile of polished rocks and fossils, a terra cotta sculpture, and many other finds worth keeping. For the most part, it would be furniture that with a bit of loving repair work could be restored and sold on at our antique market or if modern, sold at a flea market. All purchased for a very nominal sum. This served three needs: reducing waste, enjoying refurbishing our finds, and making a living.

On this visit, we had been shocked to see large amounts of refrigerators, TVs, washing machines, etc. "What is happening?" we asked the manager. "Are you turning this into a base for electrical goods?" "It's the sales," he replied. "Sales?" we repeated. "January sales. Everybody is buying new while it's cheap and dumping old models. "If you need anything here, most will still be in good working order." What a waste," Michael exclaimed, voicing my exact thoughts.

This was just another incident that made us realise how alien we felt in England, the country we had both been born in. England was hardly the tropics. Why would one need a fridge? Okay, a lot of people use milk, ice cream, meat, and fish. So did people in our parents' generation, and they did not have a fridge. We had never had a TV, preferring books. Why house a noisy washing machine, with a Laundromat nearby for sheets and towels?

That was the start of deciding it was time to think about the future and, dare I say it, settle down.

We had been living in Devon for years. When my husband died in New Zealand, Michael had been in Australia. On hearing what had happened, he sold his car for the price of an air ticket and joined me in New Zealand. My home had been on a yacht for years, sailing from Singapore. Leaving the yacht, 'Sandpiper', to be sold, Michael and I set off on a slow overland trip to England. It was time to be near our widowed Pop.

Life in England was fun at first when we bought and refurbished an old house and ran an antique market. I soon started to feel trapped; I needed to move, see more of the world, and get back to a nomadic way of life. We were free to do so after Pop passed away a month before his 98th birthday. His death affected us differently. I needed to get away and went off to East Africa for three months. After that, we often travelled to gather during the winter months. The downside to this was having to return to the same place. Owning a house gave us less freedom.

"I would like to just sell the house and spend our time travelling." Before the words were out of my mouth, I knew what the response would be. "Be your age, people in their seventies don't wander around the world as you once did; what about all your stuff?" My stuff, yes, I was caught in two worlds. While I had no desire for electrical goods and all the trappings of modern life, I was certainly not a minimalist. Over a thousand books filled the shelves, carvings collected from various places, framed paintings and drawings given to me by my artist friends, and a large collection of primate ornaments and pictures. Also, just as valuable in my eyes were beautiful shells, bits of interesting rock and driftwood, tropical seeds, fossils, and feathers.

I had slipped into the world I thought I would never want. Possessions that needed a fixed abode. The days of being able to carry all I needed in one small backpack had slipped away.

"I would like to be back in the tropics, surrounded by nature, leading a real life." "Yes, but where?" Michael responded. I did not hesitate long. "What about Sri Lanka?" I said. That was no surprise to Michael; I was always on about that country. But, as he pointed out, they were old and past experiences, and things change. "Well, they change sadly all over the world." I said. We agreed to plan for once, to go out to Sri Lanka and re-explore places I had loved and other areas before coming to a decision.

So it was that in December 2010 we boarded a plane for Sri Lanka, the island that lies like a pearl dropping from India.

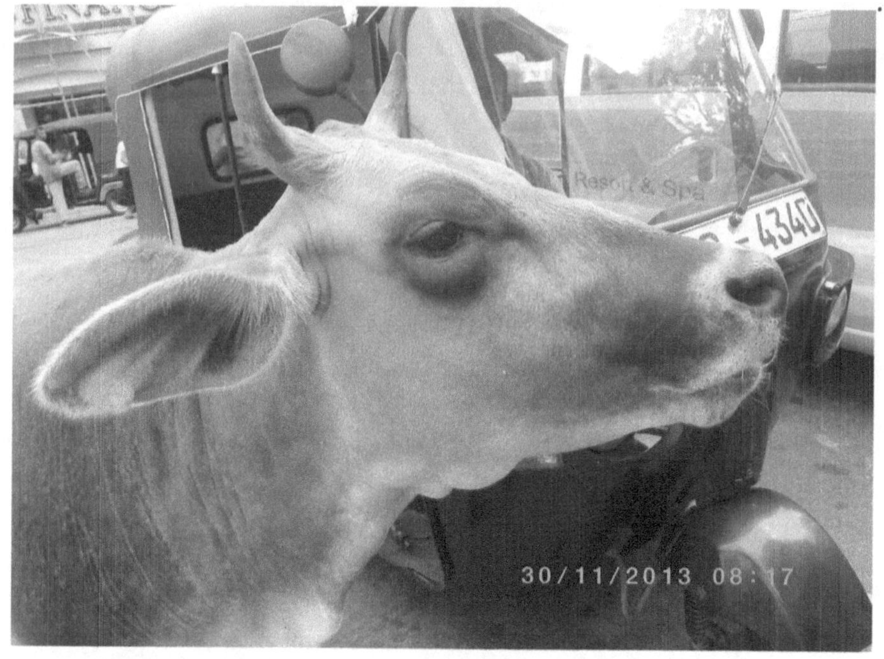

Cow and Tuk tuks

Chapter Two

Colombo and Memories From 1959

Having only small backpacks classed as hand luggage, we soon left the rest of the passengers behind as they collected their cases. No delay, our passports were stamped, giving us 30 days. A few years later, they introduced visas.

Our usual practice is to avoid cities as much as possible. Now, the plan was to revisit places I had been to before. I hoped to find the sailors' home I had stayed in in 1959.

Michael and I were both tired after the long journey and bus into Colombo. First thoughts were to find a place to spend the night. We headed for the Y.M.C.A. to find it was full. We booked into the hotel Nipon, rather grander than expected.

A gecko on the wall at once made me feel at home. Showered, we went out to find something to eat. We bought delicious rice and dhal for just Rs. 100 (about 50p). "That was about the best meal and the cheapest I have ever had," laughed Michael. At what appeared to be, until I entered, an all-male bar, we downed a stout.

I cast my mind back to 1959 when I, together with my American boyfriend, arrived in what was then Ceylon. We had been travelling together from Norway for over two years, hitchhiking and stopping to work when money ran out in many countries on the way. We crossed from India to Ceylon by ferry, a ferry which sadly no longer exists. In Anuradhapura, we became a party of three when someone gave me a baby toque monkey. Too young to be released back into the wild, we christened him Singh and continued on our way with Singh sitting happily on my backpack. We had run out of land; to discover new lands, we would have to take to the sea. On reaching Colombo, we set about trying to find a ship that would give us free passage to any place we had not yet been to, in exchange for a helping hand. It turned out no captain was interested in signing us on.

We stayed at the sailors' home, an ideal place to stay. It was inhabited mostly by European sailors who had, for various reasons, left the ship they had arrived on and were now waiting in the hope of re-joining a ship as crew. They had the advantage over us, being qualified seamen. I had wondered how hard they were trying for a passage as they were a jolly lot and had, some time before our arrival, taken part in a film being shot in Colombo as extras. The pay must have been good to keep them happy at the bar most of the day. When Don and I went seeking a ship, we left Singh on a lovely big tree in the courtyard. On our return, we would find Singh had joined the sailors at the bar, happily dipping his hand in their beer glasses. Laughing, the men would relate stories of how clever the locals were at lightening their purses. One of them had returned from seeing a movie and tried to put his hand in his back pocket for his wallet. Not only was the wallet gone, but the whole pocket had been skilfully cut out. Two had given chase, unsuccessfully, to a man on a push bike that had, in full daylight grabbed a lady's shoulder bag. While more stories were being told, one stopped to point out a visiting Captain. "See that man with a red tie, he is leaving for Hong Kong and might take you," I made my enquiry. He did not say no, just asked to see our passports. I handed them over; by then Don had joined us. One look at Don's American passport was enough. The cargo boat "Dorintha" was stopping at a port in China before continuing to Hong Kong. No American at that time would be allowed to visit China, even if listed as a seaman. This was a blow, but I had been wishing to travel alone so did not hesitate long. "OK, can Singh and I join your ship?" I think my answer was a bit of a surprise, but he said yes. I was to join the ship the following night.

With tears, hugs, and promises to keep in touch, Don and I split our money, each having $20 plus two dollars. Don said he would head back to Europe.

Next evening, I was in a very large warehouse-like shed to clear customs. There was one man behind the counter and a lone sweeper some distance away. I was asked what money I had. I produced the $20; it was handed back to me. The man went off with my passport. Singh was sitting on my lap. Suddenly, I was aware that I no longer held the note. Singh certainly had not taken it. The sweeper was still some distance away, and I was alone, the official having yet to return. When the official returned with my passport, I related what had happened. Two more men appeared, and the police were called. My backpack was searched.

The police, not unreasonably, said it must be either the official or the sweeper. Both were then searched, as was all the rubbish the sweeper had swept into a pile. Finding nothing, they said I must decide which of the two men had taken it. They would then charge him. This, of course, I refused to do, having no idea how either man could have taken it.

I still had two dollars as Singh and I climbed aboard "Dorintha". Many times in travelling, I had had less but did wish Don had kept the twenty dollars.

Did my loss and the tales the sailors told put me off Ceylon? Strangely, it did not. I found the people friendly, the motorised traffic was so little, and crossing the road could be done without looking. Many years later, I did return to Colombo with my now-late husband, Captain Bobby Moore. The same captain who had let me hitch a ride on his ship.

At that time, there was still very little in the way of traffic and we found the sailors' home. It had changed its name slightly. We went and talked to the manager. Yes, he did remember me. Well, not really, it was Singh he remembered. The tree in the courtyard still existed. The manager at the time of my visit had been just a young lad starting out on earning a living. It was good to know he had done so well. I was also happy that nothing much had changed over the long period.

Leaving my thoughts of the past, I decided it was pointless to try and find that place again. So much had changed. Had I been dropped down in Colombo without being told where I was, I would never have guessed, but then these days most cities are alike. The traffic is just as bad as in any other city. The slow pace of living that I remembered had sped up. Keen to depart, we shouldered our packs and set out for the train station.

Giant Squirrel Bee-eater

Tuk-tuk

Chapter Three

Kalutara and the Tsunami

As we moved forward to get off the train at Kalutara several ladies stopped us. It was Kalutara North. They insisted we wanted Kalutara South. Until then, we had no idea there were north and south stations. How did they know where we wished to go, we wondered, as we complied with their wishes and sat back down? Not too unexpectedly, when we got off the train at the south station, we told a Tuk-tuk driver we wanted the beach at Mermaid hotel. He said we should have got off the train at Kalutara North.

We were a little apprehensive at what we would find at this beach. Six years had passed since we were there with Pop, on Boxing Day 2004 when the Tsunami hit. We were lucky, as were all the other people in the Mermaid hotel, but we would never forget how all the small wooden buildings on the beach had been swept away. Coconut palms and Pandanus (screw-pine) were gone, or left standing on stilt-like roots, with the beach being transformed into a garbage heap. We had wondered how it could ever be cleared. No doubt it would, but would the local people be back or would we find hotels had been built in their place.

The day of the Tsunami would always stick in our minds, the horror that had devastated so many lives. When Pop passed away the following year in March, one month away from his 98th birthday, we learned from a Sri Lankan doctor that Pop's mind had been wandering, according to him. He told us that on learning the doctor was from Sri Lanka, Pop had told him that he had been to his country at the time of the Tsunami. We informed him this was no delusion on Pop's part, it was true and we were with him. No apology was forthcoming, the doctor looked a little taken aback; it appeared he did not know what to say, or perhaps what to believe.

Thinking back to that fateful day, we had breakfast and went down to the beach. Pop said he was tired and for once did not suggest going somewhere. The hotel was set back from the sea with grass, palms, and a swimming pool leading down to the beach. Michael went a little further off to sit on the grass with a book. Our rooms were the furthest from the beach. Pop and I stopped outside our rooms. I got one of the chairs from the room for him to sit on; beach loungers were not to his or our liking. With a few Resurgent magazines I intended to read, I sat on the ground with my back to the sea, talking to Pop. We were relaxed; it was just another day like any other.

Without warning, a noise I could not identify, I turned my head. My mind drew a blank, quite unable to take in what the wall of water was; then it hit us. The strength of the wave by then was not too forceful. At once, Michael was with us and a member of staff. With Michael on one side and the man taking Pop's left arm, they guided him over the steps hidden by water into his room. A room now with several inches of water covering the floor. More help came, and Pop was put in a chair which two young Sri Lankan men lifted up and carried to the floor above. Pop protesting all the way that he could walk. From there, we viewed the damage below. The sea had retreated, retreated, in fact, further than it did normally, taking much with it. I could not help fantasising that the sea was not just a body of water but had turned into a living being who, in a rage, had entered the land and taken what it could not destroy. The swimming pool, usually so clear that we could watch the kingfishers dive into it for a bath, was now full of debris, including a wooden lounger. The whole, once neat garden, was a shambles. Little remained and what did was in ruins.

I went down to our rooms; they still had a few inches of water covering the floor. Picking up my backpack, I found the films I had taken were still in their canisters but wet. I moved all things up higher in the cupboard. Returning upstairs, we were told another wave was expected, and no one was sure if the foundations would hold. Once more, with Pop still protesting that the chair he was sitting on was lifted up and carried back down to join all the other guests at the back of the hotel.

The staff were wonderful. They, no more than we, understood just what had happened, and many must have wondered how their relations were faring. We were all in rather a state of shock, not understanding what had happened, and I doubt if any of us realised that this was not just a local happening but covered such a wide area and taken so many lives.

Some days previously, we had taken a Tuk-tuk to some wetlands to watch birds, with Pop wishing to experience a ride in this novel vehicle. We had an enjoyable time. The driver picked us water lilies and made necklaces of the flowers for us. We were able to spot many kinds of water birds. Pop enjoyed himself and was pleased with his ride but said he was a little too tall at 6'3" and would not be doing it again. We bought a Tuk-tuk model for him as a souvenir.

Now, as we stood with the others at the back of the hotel, the conversation around us was Naturally speculations on what had happened. Local staff were no more enlightened than we were, and I do not recall that any of us mentioned the word 'tsunami'. Perhaps if anyone had, it would not have been a word that meant anything to us at the time. Later, we heard or read that a warning had been sent to Colombo saying that a tsunami was coming and giving a time. A taxi was sent to the airport. True or not, it should be taken as a warning to make such messages clear.

We did not stay outside for long. Our Tuk-tuk driver, who had taken us to the wetlands, arrived and said he would take us to his grandmother's, where we would be safe.

Off we went, over the rail track to grandmother's village. A delightful place where we would have been happy to have visited at any time. Small houses nestled among the many trees on which we could see a number of colourful birds. The whole scene had a wonderfully comfortable feel about it, reminiscent of Malay kampongs. The villagers appeared to be as pleased to welcome us as we were to be with them. Pop stole the show with the ladies; bringing out the best chair for him. He was wearing bedroom slippers and socks. Both these items were now soaked. Swiftly, taking a foot each, they removed his footwear and put them in the sun to dry. Tea was then served. We watched with amazement as a pretty young girl held a cup of tea and started spooning it into Pop's mouth. They must have noticed his slightly shaky hand. Pop always protested at any help not asked for and was very independent. This time he sat back, opening his mouth like a good child as the spoon came forward. No disgust showed on his face, though if the tea was like ours it was very strong with sugar. Perhaps he thought it was all a local custom. Later we asked how he enjoyed his tea. "Is that what it was, tasted very sweet," was his reply.

The doors of the houses were open. There were TV sets turned on, showing the very scenes of huge waves and destruction we had witnessed. Still thinking all we had seen was only local, it was a surprise to see it being shown on the television so soon.

Michael and I were also seated on chairs in the open. Dramatic as the pictures on the screen were, everyone's attention, especially the children's, was directed at us. They did not stand and stare as in Some places but set out to entertain us. A boy got half a coconut shell and filled it with water and put a bit of wood in. Then, with a hollow twig, he kept stirring it, making a froth. Then, using the stick, he blew bubbles. Smaller boys copied, not always with success. We all laughed and clapped. They picked fruit for us and plied us with water and tea.

Things had been organised in a remarkably short time. Information was received in the afternoon that no more waves would come. Adjunda, our Tuk-tuk driver, returned to take us back to the hotel. We had removed all our stuff to the floor above and had to share a room. As others did, we decorated the veranda with all our wet clothes. When we arrived back, helicopters were flying overhead, and uniformed men with clipboards were assessing the damage. Our hotel had not suffered like others. Only the end room nearest to the beach was damaged. This was due to the design; two long strips of bedrooms bridged at the top end by the upper-story restaurant. The open part under the restaurant allowed the sea to flow through. The only difference in the dining service was the lack of linen serviettes. The laundry was flooded. The staff were quite amazing, saying it would all be back to normal in five days and were already clearing the pool.

All guests were accounted for. Just one family, parents with a teenage daughter, had been caught on the beach and pushed against a chain-link fence. They were helped and brought to safety by an unknown local man. The girl's arm was hurt, but she still smiled.

There was a TV in a room off the restaurant. We crowded in and learned that we had witnessed a tsunami that was far from local. So many countries were affected and thousands were dead. How lucky we had been. We felt guilty for having enjoyed our time in the village while so much suffering was going on. We were all now subdued but affected in different ways. One Englishman had a mobile phone and had phoned someone to let them know he was OK. He informed us all of the unbelievable fact that the man he phoned was still in bed and knew nothing about the danger he had been in. Hardly surprisingly, with the time difference, at about eight-thirty in the morning of Boxing Day in the UK. One young man lost all his diving equipment. This he related as if it was the worst tragedy of the day. He said he had had enough and was getting out of the country as soon as possible. Another man pointed out he still had his life, unlike many others. He was young and strong and could so easily have stayed and helped. A girl appeared and asked what all the noise was about. She was on the floor above and had slept through it all until being woken by all the noise. The Tsunami had hit about nine in the morning. She thought it was unbelievable that anyone would be up at nine in the morning on holiday. We learned that a train running between Colombo and Galle had been swept off the tracks, not so far south of us near Hikkaduwa. Thousands had died; it was hard to take in, and we all felt a little stunned.

People were talking of leaving, but gas stations had suffered so little transport to be had, and many roads were closed. All these inconveniences were nothing compared to what thousands had suffered. We worried about the local people. Sandy, a beach boy who had a van and had given us a far better time than the local travel agent at the hotel had tried to talk us into, and at a fraction of the cost. Sandy, when we found him, was okay, and as his van had been inland at the time, was fine, but he had lost his home. He told us the man with the monkey called Martin (the monkey's name, not the man) was okay, as was his family of pets. He also thought that the man we had purchased pictures and sarongs from was okay.

That morning after the tsunami was when we felt the real impact of the tragedy. Trying to find out about people we had slightly known. We tend to feel more empathy for people we have met, even if for a short time, than others who are just numbers.

Michael paced the distance from the hotel to the beach, 150 paces. How fortunate we had been. A local catamaran was lodged in the sands of a coconut palm that still stood upright, looking as if it had stood on tiptoe and caught the catamaran as it passed. All the interesting little shacks that had once been homes or businesses were gone. We had walked down the beach on Christmas Day morning, and two ladies with a few little girls had greeted us with "HAPPY CHRISTMAS." We gave them the pieces of Christmas cake the hotel staff had placed by our beds. Where were they now? We came to what had been a well-constructed souvenir shop. Only two days before we had been chatting with the owner as he sat carving outside his shop. The shop had been full of batiks, carvings and other items. Now, while the remains of the building were just recognizable, the man sitting outside no longer had his happy smile. He had lost everything. Even his tools had been taken by the sea, as had his entire stock. Among the debris that covered the sand, we saw a dead chicken, two rabbits and a goat. Perhaps they had been someone's pets. Animals that were wild or not caged or restricted in some way had, we were told, sensed the coming danger and gone inland before the first wave appeared. Clever as we humans tend to think we are, there is a lot we could learn from other animals.

We left the beach and came back along the road. A very subdued line of people was making their way up the hill to the temple where they would receive food and be able to sleep. A wire cage, broken but with a budgie nesting box attached, lay on its side. Three dead birds and a coiled python at the bottom were still alive, having had their fill of dead birds. A rustling sound and a monitor lizard entered a broken pipe. At the hotel, the water tank was being filled. People from surrounding homes lined up with buckets for water; their wells had all been polluted.

We had taken items of our clothing and packed them up with some money for Adjunda. He was away trying to get fuel. We gave them to his father and brother who were where Adjunda usually had his Tuk-tuk. Later, Adjunda came to the hotel full of thanks for our little gift.

That evening, we were due to leave as scheduled but were told to be prepared not to if no transport to the airport could be found. A minibus arrived to take us and some girls who were going to Colombo. It was the east and south of the island that had suffered so badly in the tsunami; we had been lucky to be further north even so as we got to Bentota, just north of Kalutara, we witnessed flattened buildings and piles of wood and broken furniture from what had once been a furniture shop.

At the airport, we had requested assistance for Pop, which meant a wheelchair rather than a long walk. Now, many young people were more in need of assistance - broken legs, arms, etc. It looked like an airlift for the war wounded. Pop was able to walk and did so.

Now, six years later, our minds in the past, we made our way to Mermaid Hotel beach. We were amazed to find everything looking as it had before the tsunami... Well, not quite, the foundations of a hotel near to the Mermaid which had been washed away had gone for good. The grounds of the hotel looked as before, palms and pandanus, fully grown and looking just as we remembered them before that fateful day. Wooden buildings were along the beach but not as many as before. We looked in vain for the souvenir shop. We asked the local people but none had been there before the tsunami and knew nothing of it. Asking after Sandy who had taken us on trips in his van, one person knew his phone number and phoned him, and he appeared. We were happy to learn that things were turning out well for him. We contemplated going in and having a drink in the grounds of the Mermaid Hotel, remembering how the palm squirrels used to beg fruit from us. Or to go round the back and see if the weaver bird still had a nest there and the babblers, birds we christened "car park birds". Happy memories we would keep, no need to try and recreate.

Amilo, our driver for the day, told us that after the tsunami, the beach had been cleared but the local people, who had lived and made a business there, no longer wish to be near the sea. Who can blame them? The government had built a village inland for them. He drove us around, pointing out mongoose and monitors, then to his parents' house where his father pressed us to spend the night. It overlooked the sea, with one room and a veranda. A night spent there would be interesting and a financial help to him and his wife. We then, as agreed, went off to buy vegetables for the meal they would cook us. We attempted to purchase from the stalls, but Amilo insisted we go to the rather unattractive supermarket.

They had digital scales but when I selected three large carrots, which I felt was more than enough, three more were added to make up the weight, they said. What we found more annoying was that they insisted on putting each of the items we bought in their own separate plastic bag. About 30 years ago, when having come from Singapore, I gave someone a plastic bag. They were delighted and returned with fruit as a gift. Plastic has its uses but far more misuses and will eventually, indirectly, kill us all if we do not start doing something about it very soon. After a long drive, Amilo took us to his home of which he was, I am sure, rightly very proud. It was well inland and, as he said, safe from any tsunami should one happen again. It was new and modern. Tiled floor and windows with shutters. We met his beautiful wife and his two-year-old son. The latter did not think much of us at first but became better disposed when we took his photo. Furnished with a couch and armchairs and a TV. Also, an electric sewing machine. I noticed a treadle machine had been discarded to a corner of the house. We were then asked if we would not prefer to stay at his house. Honesty made us say yes, it was more conventional and inland which we prefer to the sea, but we had promised his parents so did not wish to change plans; it was, after all, only one night. The food we had brought had been made into a tasty meal on our return. We agreed the bathroom was unexpectedly new and modern. Loo, washbasin and shower. What it lacked was a door, also a window; a large square hole in the wall was obviously made for a window. In all, it was hardly private as it was in the courtyard where other people milled about. Fortunately, we were left alone. That I could stand, what I did dislike was the stairs. Leading up to the room and veranda. This was by way of cement steps, fine in themselves, but after the first few against the house wall, there was nothing but thin air on both sides. Handrails, even if only on one side, would have been nice but no doubt thought unnecessary.

We ate on the balcony, with the sea in front viewed through waving palms. Amilo's father – very rarely, when being introduced to a family member, are you told their name. Usually just "My father, sister, cousin, etc." The Father showed us his coin collection. Having nothing but local coins at the time, we mailed him some from the UK. Whether they arrived or not, we never knew. After we had agreed that it was very peaceful and had told him we were thinking of returning one day to live in Sri Lanka, he suggested we could have his house for Rs15,000, about £75 per month. His son had told us he paid Rs. 8000 rent for his house. As an inducement, he said he would have a door put on the bathroom, with no mention of handrails on the steps. The house consisted of just one room at the top of the stairs without rails, to which the veranda was attached. That, as it turned out, was ours for the night. A double bed, judging by the items around, was the parents' bedroom. After breakfast, we paid him Rs. 1000 and then extra for his wife's cooking. It had been an experience that we could afford. We would not be taking up his offer. We were all happy as we said goodbye, and Amilo drove us to the station.

Next stop, Ambalangoda. Not a place we had ever been to before. We met a man on the train who had been to Jersey, Channel Islands, to study French. He was then a French teacher, had perfect English, and said he also spoke German. We felt like hanging our heads in shame at such linguistic achievements. We told him we wanted to visit a turtle place that saved injured turtles and also kept turtle eggs until hatched to release them with a better chance of survival. Our friend insisted we must see the lake and its islands, also the moonstone mines, where he assured us was the only place in the world where blue moonstones could be found. Then of course, we must see Asia's longest reclining Buddha statue. We could hire a Tuk-tuk to take us to all these places and then for just Rs. 900, we could stay at Lachman. We took his word and found a very obliging Tuk-tuk driver, Chaminda. The mines were not what we expected, just large holes in the ground, down which a man came up with a basket of sand, which was then washed in a puddle. We were shown two very small bits of what looked like mother of pearl; he said they were moonstones. The next step was seeing a man polishing some good-sized stones and an assortment of uncut gems. All this was viewed for free. Now, having widened our knowledge of the wonders of moonstones, we were politely but firmly invited into the shop to see some very beautiful jewellery in the hope we would buy. I asked to use their loo.

We enjoyed the lagoon the most with its islands. On Cinnamon Island, government-owned, the caretaker showed us how he prepares the bark before drying. This is now a very familiar sight but at that time neither Michael nor I had seen it done before. Taking a stick of the cinnamon tree, he shaved the thin outer cover of the bark and rubbed it down with a copper tube. With a sharp knife, he cut lightly into the bark, drew it down, and stripped the resulting bark off the stick. This was then put on a rack to dry. We were offered a packet to buy. We gave a donation instead. When travelling, we refuse to carry anything that is not essential. Back on the boat, we were watching birds when a young girl in a boat paddled up and showed us a wee monkey, a baby purple-faced leaf monkey *Semnopithecus vetulus velulus*. We were told it had fallen from a tree and was about a week old. I hoped it would survive. It was a real darling. That it had fallen out of the tree is unlikely as it would have been hanging tightly to its mother. The more likely answer is that a new male had taken over the troop and had tried to kill all the young to make sure all future babies would be his. If this was the case, it was strange and most fortunate that this little chap was not injured in any way. We were able to watch his relations in the trees.

One island was populated, with a school and a Buddhist temple that we were able to visit. As usual, a monk tied a thread round our wrists for luck, his or ours, not sure, as he was not slow in asking for a donation. The best part was when going up the temple steps; we came face to face with a giant squirrel *Ratufa macroura*. We were told he was begging for bananas but think it really wanted its photo taken.

Back on board, we watched a white-bellied fish eagle *Haliaeetus leucogaster* flying overhead, a little cormorant *Phalacrocorax niger*, and the bright blue kingfisher *Halcyon smyrnensis* sitting on a branch overhanging the water, head to one side, waiting for a suitable fish to pass by. On overhead wires sat, waiting to be admired, the beautiful Blue-tailed Bee-eater *Merops philippinus*. In the water swam enormous water monitors *Varanus salvator*, about two meters long, looking like prehistoric animals. A tree called balsa by the boatman, but not as we know balsa, was in bloom with white flowers contrasting with its incredibly round green poisonous fruit. Snake Island was pointed out to us, so-called because any snakes found on islands where people inhabited were removed to this island. Did they find the food they required and survive? The boatman assured us they did, but we did wonder if any survey had been done. Our one-and-a-half-hour boat trip came to an end, leaving us well satisfied.

We then went to Kosgoda to the Sea Turtle Hatchery. This hatchery had been destroyed in the tsunami but was now working again. Sri Lanka is fortunate in hosting many kinds of turtles who come to its beaches to lay eggs. It is not only turtles that are attracted by the sandy beaches. Tourists, dogs, and local people who dig the eggs up to eat or sell to be eaten all take their toll on the declining turtle population. Now the turtle egg collectors are being paid to bring the eggs to the hatchery, where they are reburied in mounds with notices, like graves with headstones, giving the date and type of turtle so they know when to expect the eggs to hatch. When hatched they are put into concrete tanks, before being taken out to sea and avoiding birds, dogs and anything that might fancy a little turtle snack. They said out of a whole clutch of eggs only one will be female. What we have learned is that it depends on the temperature the eggs are kept at that determines the sex of the turtle. Some of the turtles are born with defects, possibly owing to manmade pollution. Blind ones, others with distorted shells and they had two albino green turtles *Chelonian mydas*. Apparently the albinos would not live long but be taken by sharks. I doubted that a white turtle would attract a shark any more than his regular-coloured brothers. All these turtles are kept, the blind ones being fed by hand. All six types of turtles come to Sri Lanka to lay eggs. Loggerhead *Cacvaretta*. Hawksbill *Eretmochelys imbricata*. The flesh of this is said to be poisonous; unhappily, this has not stopped it from becoming endangered as this is the turtle that is caught and combs jewellery and other items sold as tortoiseshell are made from its shell. Rather late in the day, this has been brought to the attention of countries and people are now discouraging the buying of tortoiseshell. With many countries making it illegal to import any such items. A small turtle Olive Ridley *Lepidochelys olivacea* is endangered owing to poaching for its flesh and being caught in the trawling fish nets. The leatherback *Dermochelys coriacea* not in the hatchery is by far the largest of all the turtles and while its flesh is not eaten its eggs are. Jellyfish are its main food and now with all the plastic bags we humans so thoughtlessly dump, the turtle does not realise the floating plastic bag will not feed it but kill it. We did feel that the tanks these exhibits were housed in were a far cry from the ocean and could have been deeper. On the whole, it's a good project and educational.

Hanging on to our seats, we bumped along in our Tuk-tuk on a very uncared-for side road to see the longest reclining Buddha statue in Asia. We might have passed on this if other people had not pressed us to visit it. All over the world, places, rivers, buildings, etc., are described as being the longest, shortest, highest, lowest, and so on. Mostly, it does not mean that the place or item is the best. Judging this statue on its artistic merits alone, we were not impressed, nor were we very impressed at being told it was VERY old and then saying 200 years. Perhaps they had left a zero off. The restoration it had undergone was more impressive. We were told that apart from the statue, the whole place had been crumbling away. Repainting is still going on with scaffolding up, enabling painters to repaint the very ornate ceiling. At either end of the passage, in front of the Buddha, were more interesting three-dimensional groups, one end depicting Tamils out for war, and opposite, more peaceful Sinhalese. One did not have to wonder which race dreamed that up. All very garish but fun, and along the wall stretched many identical Buddha statues. Pictured below were people, a devil, and a lion. As it is so well off the beaten track, it's doubtful they get many visitors. The tiny monk who had taken our money, only Rs. 250 entrance fee, handed us the huge key, weighing a kilo.

The mask museum, though interesting, turned out to be a large shop. Some good carving, but we were not there to buy and by then having enjoyed a full and enjoyable day, both Michael and I felt very tired. Chaminda, our driver, treated us to the most refreshing drink of a king coconut and some green mango before returning us to Lachman who later served up a splendid dinner with numerous curry dishes. His place was new as his first building, when just a year old, had been swept away in the tsunami. Believing that disaster does not strike in the same place twice, he had rebuilt on the edge of the beach. We met his son, twice the size of his father, and their dog with half a front leg and a bad patch on its back, another victim of the tsunami. We both agreed Sri Lanka was turning out to be all we hoped. We slept well that night.

Jambo Fruit

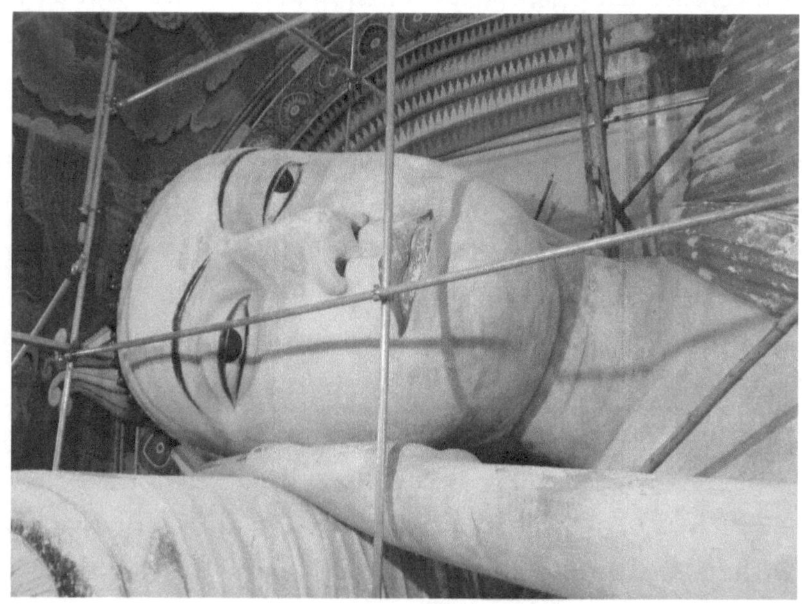

Buddha under restoration

Chapter Four

Galle - People from the Past

We were now in the place that had perhaps influenced me in choosing Sri Lanka above all the other countries.

A couple of days before Christmas 1978, Bobby, my late husband, Pixie, our monkey, and Bob-tail, her cat, sailed into Galle harbour on our yacht "Sandpiper." We spent about two wonderful months refurbishing our boat and meeting friends, the main one being Don Windsor and his wife Prema, who welcomed all crew from yachts that entered Galle. We celebrated Christmas in his home and many other days and special occasions. We visited Unawatuna, then undiscovered by tourists, and stayed in a little palm-thatched hut. Before we left, our dinghy was kidnapped, and we paid a ransom to get it back.

Our stay in Galle in 1978 was full of interest, and we voted it the best place we had stayed in our cruising. A detailed description of our time in Galle can be found in 'MONKEYING AROUND AT SEA'.

We made our way to Galle Fort and, by lucky chance, stopped at 'Beach Haven' planning to stay a few nights. Our choice of accommodation could not have been better. To this day, we still visit Sita and her relations, having become almost part of the wonderful family. At that time, we had chosen them purely by luck and were very happy that they were proving so friendly and helpful.

I had lost contact with Don Windsor and his family years before and after the Tsunami had written in the hope that the family was all right. His son, Santosh, had replied. Sad news - both Don and Prema, his wife, had passed away many years before. Walking around the Fort, I found it more crowded than I remembered. Tourists were swelling the population, and shops catering to them, and so many jewellers. Do people really come on holiday and buy jewellery? Apparently, yes. Coming out of the Fort, we wanted to go to the fruit market. A tuk-tuk approached us; he was very insistent, saying he would take us anywhere we like for a small sum. We like walking to really see the places we visit, but then agreed and let him take us to the market.

We had arranged to meet Santosh and I wished to see the port. The next day we stepped out and happened to meet the same Tuk-tuk driver we had used the day before, easily recognizable by his one remaining tooth. We asked to be taken to the port. Approaching the port, he asked us if we had a boat. Replying in the negative, I also added that I had once had a boat there in 1979. Sunil then introduced himself, telling me that he worked there then. "What was the name of my boat?" "Sandpiper," I told him. He remembered, perhaps not so much me or my late husband, but of course Pixie, who actually had not been very friendly to him when he worked for us. He mentioned an Italian boat and others I remembered. How strange that the first Tuk-tuk we had taken turned out to be driven by someone that I once long ago knew. Things at the port had changed a lot, and it was not possible to get in without a permit. I had wanted to see where we had spent several months so happily. Sunil said he would take us to the house where we had spent so many enjoyable evenings and meet Santosh, who now ran a business for the port. It was strange going up to the gate that I had been through with my husband and Pixie many times long ago.

When we met Santosh, he set about getting us a permit to visit the port. This gave us plenty of time to look around. It had changed; I would not have known the place. I looked at the patio of the house. Did we really have the Christmas party there with so many people? It looked so small. I asked about the effect of the tsunami. No one had been in the house at the time, and only one servant had died. The patio that looked so small was not the one I remembered, as much of the house was damaged and had to be rebuilt. It no longer had a delightful garden, as opposite the entrance had been built the offices where we waited for a permit. The permits came, and we were taken around the docks. All was changed. Since the tsunami, the facility for taking yachts out of the water no longer exists. Japanese had rebuilt one only suitable for fishing boats. One yacht on that fateful day in 2004 had headed out to sea. The rest of the yachts were tossed ashore and smashed. But all the occupants were ashore and suffered no loss of life. It was kind of Santosh to have bothered with us; he appeared very busy but kindly drove us back to Beach Haven. So I had seen the place that had meant so much to me now very changed. The past that I was looking for here no longer existed.

As we wandered along the Fort Ramparts, it was clear that this was now a tourist destination. We were asked to give money, and a young man would fling himself off a cliff into the sea below. "You get a good photo," we were told. This was the last thing we would donate to, supposing something went wrong and we had sent him to his death. We walked on, declining an offer to buy very old coins found in a wreck. We sat and chatted with a lady selling lace-edged tablecloths. She told us the Fort hosted five stray dogs, all vaccinated, who played happily along the beach and looked well cared for.

The Fort had not suffered in the tsunami, but the residents, in particular the family at Beach Haven, had helped with food, etc. Visiting the Maritime and Archaeology Museum, we saw a large model of an old Dutch boat that had sunk many years before, a display of pots, etc., recovered from the wreck, and a few pieces found on the beach after the tsunami that are believed to have come from Indonesia. Then we were shown a movie about recovering wreck treasure. One wreck had been mapped and covered with netting. Two days later, the tsunami had come and taken back all the items removed. A shiver went down my spine.

That evening, we discovered the Royal Dutch Café on Lyn Bann Street. Here, Fazal not only cooked us food we enjoyed but also told stories and generally entertained us, making it a place to visit almost daily when in Galle.

Before leaving England, I had contacted a friend, Terry, who is now living in England, to tell her that we were going to Sri Lanka, knowing she also loved the place. We had met many years ago in Lumut, Malaysia, when she and her husband, Gerald, came to the yacht club on weekends where they had a day sailor. We were on "Sandpiper," and I was invited to visit their lovely home and experience something I had been missing for a long time: a real bathroom with fresh water. Their two little boys were fascinated with Pixie. As we both loved travelling, we had kept in touch, though we had only met once since 1978.

Before I could tell her why I had phoned, she excitedly told me she was going to Sri Lanka to look at houses that were for sale. She too planned on moving out here. We contacted each other again in Galle. Terry's son, Tristan, was flying out from Dubai, and we all had lunch together.

This was not the only person from England whom we were to meet so many miles away. On learning of our proposed trip, Cousin Sue had phoned and told us that her son, Brian, was in Unawatuna where he and his wife had built a beach bar some time ago, called B's Bar. We had met Brian just once before at his grandfather's funeral, who was also our uncle. It seemed that Sri Lanka was a place that brought friends and relations together.

Michael and I agreed that so far, although the country had changed, it did appear to be the place we were looking for. At breakfast the following morning, we were joined by a German girl, here as a volunteer vet in Kandy. Her horror stories shocked us. She told of vets who would fix a dog for an owner but not properly, so they would come back to do it again and get paid. Muslim men she had witnessed being very cruel to animals. Worse was to come. Chinese were caught killing dogs and even going to rescue centres to buy the fattest dog to eat. I felt ill. Chinese I was well aware of being a very cruel race in general and that they ate dogs. Also, a friend had told me that a friend of hers had been coming to holiday in Sri Lanka but no longer as there were so many Chinese. We so far had not seen a single Chinese. The German girl said she could enjoy Sri Lanka but was shocked after finding how things were with animals here even though a Buddhist country. MGOs were not made very welcome as some people had come under that title after the tsunami and bought land and even brought in guns to sell to the Tamils. We had sadly heard that many that had come to help had turned out to be helping themselves in various ways.

One of the reasons I loved Sri Lanka was the empathy they had with animals. This was based on my experience many years ago of how Pixie was treated. Admittedly, the people we knew were all Buddhists, but how could a country with a Buddhist majority allow such things to happen on such a scale? This was the first worrying thing we had come across so far.

The first night I had seen a closed door I wanted to photograph. Since then, we had been looking for it, but it had vanished. By chance, we entered an antique shop. Upon entering the open door, there it was - the door I had wanted to photograph. The owner allowed us to close the door and take a photo. I remember someone telling us that December was the dry season. Rain kept tipping down.

After a few days, we had seen all the places of interest in the Fort. It was time now to move on and see other places that neither of us had been to. First, a short ride to Unawatuna to see Brian. 'B's Place' was not easy to find. Knowing it was right on the beach, we tried walking along but while bars, etc. continued, the beach did not. When we finally found it very near where we started, Brian was out, not so the sea that lapped the stilts of his beach bar. His partner Asoka gave us a beer and told us how until this year they had had sand but something had happened and they had lost their beach. A few years later things had changed again and his end of the beach had sand, the other end had lost it. Blame was put on the breakwater that had been erected. Meetings were held and naturally the end with the beach wished things to remain. The other end wanted their beach back. The breakwater was dismantled and the beach reseeded. Now the bay is back as it had been before man's interference, a long curve of sand reaching the full length of the bay. We booked at the Village Inn; we would see Brian the following day and meanwhile decided to walk to the Japanese Peace Pagoda. The walk started out on a hard surface but not for long. The rain had stopped but the ground was muddy, we lost the track amidst huge boulders and gushing water. An elderly man caught up with us and loaned me his stick, guiding us through the torrent of water, fun but tiring. The Pagoda was finally reached, we climbed the steps carefully not waking the many sleeping dogs and walked around admiring the view. Perhaps owing to the weather, we had seen little wildlife. We finished our walk around the pagoda when we noticed a paved road leading from it and a tuk-tuk discharged its passengers. Then down came the rain. The ride back was easy.

That evening, we went in search of dinner. If one ate seafood, that would have been easy. We found a vegetarian restaurant. The menu was not very appealing, with veggie burgers, etc. Further along was another vegetarian place with more attractive local food; they even had beer. For some reason, beer is not advertised, and it is hit and miss if they serve it. We sat drinking a beer with an Irish/Englishman, a couple of years younger than Michael. He told us he had flu and had suffered badly even though he had had anti-flu injections. The owner joined us. We knew him; he had given us directions on the path to the Pagoda. He was married to a local girl and enjoying life there. Our first lesson in Sinhala – the word for eggplant: WAMBOTU.

We met Brian the next morning, so like his mother, he was easily recognizable. He was very enthusiastic. A little worried about what former guests would think when they came for Christmas and found the beach gone. His wife, Kay, was coming out with a friend. They were both still working in the UK, aiming to be able to retire in Sri Lanka one day. Brian was seriously trying to learn the language.

Leaving Brian, we caught a bus to Marissa. Passing the fishermen sitting on stilts in the sea near Ahangama. We hoped to meet up again with Terry in Mirissa and went to a place she had been told of. Amarasinghe guest house was set in a delightful garden which also boasted monkeys, peacocks, and butterflies along with charming owners. The evening meal was communal on long tables with a very large assortment of curries. The next day when we walked to the beach, the rain was still with us. An old lady invited us into shelter, her daughter arrived and acted as an interpreter while mother chewed beetle. The walk to the guest house was part of the attraction, the path going alongside a river. Stopping to photograph a bird, we noticed a wonderful lizard in its brightly coloured mating costume. Monkeys were having fun high in the trees. As we walked, we stopped many times to admire a strange or colourful insect.

That night at dinner, I met an interesting French lady. She took out a plastic bag in which she deposited half of her dinner; she was feeding a stray dog, so we donated some of our meal to this worthy cause. We learned that she had spent most of her life in India. Her only daughter lived in Australia and was expecting her first child at the age of 43. This was stated as a fact, and we were not quite sure if it was with approval.

The rain continued falling in sheets, confining us to our room with the door open from which we escaped now and then in the brief intervals when it stopped to squelch round the garden. Khemin, an Englishman we had chatted to, was on his rather superior patio with his neighbours, a young couple who, like us, also turned out to be brother and sister. At first, we took them to be locals, that is until they spoke. They were born in Australia with parents originating from Sri Lanka. This was their first visit to the country to bring the ashes of their father to scatter in a cemetery in Colombo. The afternoon passed pleasantly as we chatted, finding we all had things in common. Khemin, of our generation, lived in a Buddhist retreat and like us, did not have a TV. The Australians found this strange. Except for the brother, we were all vegetarians. Having been born in Australia, the young couple spoke only English; Khemin was interested in the fact that we were considering making Sri Lanka our home. He asked many questions, most of which we had not given a thought to. Michael was not very talkative, having a tooth that was worrying him and feeling cold. When the rain stopped, we retired to our room and Michael covered himself with all the clothes that were not wet, which was not very much. An excellent evening meal made Michael feel much better.

Bidding our friends goodbye the following morning, we made our way down the muddy track to catch a bus to Matara. Luck was with us when we no sooner arrived at the bus stop than an express bus to Matara pulled up. We did not have to stand, getting seats next to each other. Our destination was the bank, funds having run dry. No waiting to get served, but it took half an hour to exchange our dollars for a large wad of rupee notes. Armed with money, we caught another bus to Tangalla and a tuk-tuk to the Kingfisher. Here the beach was clean and very few tourists. We had a beer with a couple from Yorkshire and shared experiences. They mentioned having a good evening in Unawatuna at 'B's Place'. On being told that he was the son of our cousin, they said they would play a trick on him next time they visited and asked us his mother's name and the names of his brothers. We expected they would set themselves up as fortune tellers but never heard the outcome. Walking along the promenade with the sea dashing itself against reef and rocks, a man approached us and told us to visit his son's art gallery. Doing as bid, we found the gallery full of exciting paintings in a new but small studio. Most of his paintings were lost in the Tsunami. The salvaged ones bore the marks of their rescue from the sea. He had had exhibitions in various European countries, and they were much better than the few local paintings we had seen so far. When I saw a painting of two toque monkeys, I had to have it, plus one of his postcards depicting a monkey and tiger. These were to add to my primate picture collection in the UK of about 80 pictures, now donated to the Ape and Monkey sanctuary in Wales. Michael, feeling much better, went for a walk while I sat on the rocks watching the sea. A man with a platform right on the edge of the water said he could make us rice and curry that night. He set up a table and chairs, and a Swedish man joined us for a very pleasant evening.

Our main reason for stopping at Tangala was to do some bird watching. Michael got up before six and went off with his camera, while I, for some reason, slept solidly until seven. Michael returned, happy with some photos of various birds, but had missed the best shot of all, a kingfisher. He assured me it would have been a prize photo had he taken it.

When travelling, we always try to stay at locally owned places, but that morning we discovered a German owned the place we had chosen to stay. So much for supporting local places. In the harbour were hundreds of colourful fishing boats, but we found we could not walk along the beach to them owing to a river crossing the path. We enjoyed pottering around, seeing many birds and monitor lizards, and without really noticing, had got right into the harbour. This was brought to our attention when we wanted to leave by the main entrance and were told we should not have got in without a pass. How we had got in we honestly could not tell, having been too busy photographing birds to notice. We toured the town and market trying to buy a pair of shades, Michael having lost his. None were to be found, not too surprising as we did not see anyone wearing them. Lunch was a King coconut drink and the jelly, a banana, and a mango.

Later in the day, we retraced Michael's steps, still looking for the lost shades. I sat on some rocks where the top was completely flat and covered in grass that looked as if it had just been carefully cut.

Returning along the lagoon, we found a place for curry and dhal and sat watching the sun sink below the horizon as flocks of noisy parakeets flew into the palms for the night.

I found Michael's lost shades, neatly put in their case in his pack. His worries were not over; he then trod on a dead sea urchin on the beach. He was fortunate that the spines in his foot pulled out easily. The night before, I had made friends with a black dog and her two brown puppies. The next night, they greeted us, but we had nothing to give them.

Naughty Young female elephant.

Peacock

Grey Langur. The monkey usually called Hanuman.

Chapter Five

Yala National Park - Looking for Leopards

The next stop was Tissamanarama. What a mouthful! We were relieved to find that even local people referred to it as Tissa. People had told us this was the best place to stop if we wanted to take a safari in Yala National Park. There was certainly no shortage of people offering to take us. Vikum Lodge turned out to be a good choice to stay, very clean, friendly, and they would arrange the trip to the N.P. It was also up for sale. Four years later, we were to stay again with friends there. New owners who also wished to sell but now very dirty and uncared for, and even the delightful garden had deteriorated. In hindsight, we should have gone to the park that afternoon with another couple and shared expenses. To see a leopard was high on our list, and we felt we had a much better chance of seeing one early in the morning. That evening over dinner, the same couple told us how lucky they had been; they had seen a leopard. Our afternoon had not been wasted. We had walked to Tissa Wewa, a man-made lake; all such lakes here are confusingly called tanks. An island in the centre looked like a meeting place for birds. Pelicans, Egrets, Ibis, and cormorants were enjoying a peaceful existence away from humans, surrounded by water containing all they needed in the way of food.

A number of coaches full of local families were out for the day. They stopped by the river and bathed before tucking into the rice and curry they had with them. We headed to a large white dagoba, with the usual stone elephants guarding it. There we were asked both for money and food, something that had not happened before. The highlight was seeing, just as we were leaving, a small dark elephant carrying palm leaves.

Returned to our lodge and enjoyed the garden. An employer came up and handed us a wee tortoise with a smooth but patterned shell. We replaced him in a flower bed; he stayed still until we looked away and then he vanished. Nadin, the driver that the Lodge had provided for us, had seen a Dutch couple go into a very expensive hotel. He thought they might join us the next morning. The hotel would not let the local man in. We had seen this before and also signs saying 'Europeans Only'.

Was this an old colonial habit? Michael and I both agreed that we would not entertain going into a place that would not allow its own citizens to enter.

Michael went to the hotel and saw the couple, but they were not interested in joining us. At dusk, we saw our first hare, *Lepus nigricollis*, in the garden.

The next morning was to be the day we would see a leopard, so we told ourselves. Ready to go at 4:30 am, it was rather disappointing that Nalin was less keen and did not appear until five. In the dark, the ride to the park was much longer than expected. Just before entering the park, a hare crossed our path. We had never seen one before the previous night. After lightening our purse considerably, the park guide joined us. By then, it was light and the park appeared full of peacocks. One evidently rather fancied us. We had to stop in the middle of the track while it displayed, pivoting round, giving us an all-round view. Beautiful but a proper show-off. The small herd of elephants we saw were all female. One young one made us laugh when she kept challenging us, doing a little dance in front of us. When she lifted her foot and placed it, none too lightly, on the front of the vehicle, our driver was not amused and shouted and banged the side of his door. Having got this response from us, she backed off and went on her way.

We had said how we really wanted to see a leopard but rather regretted it later as we kept driving to places where not only was there no leopard to be seen but very little wildlife of any kind. So we then asked to see monkeys, pigs, and crocodiles. This was easily done; we saw a number of Hanuman Langur (*Presbytis entellus*). Also, a few Purple-faced leaf monkeys, (*Presbytis senex*). Enjoying watching them, I kept forgetting to take a photo when the best opportunities were presented. Then we enjoyed watching a sounder of wild pigs *Sus scrofa* who went about their business as if they knew just where they were going and what they were doing, not giving us a second glance. The spotted deer *Cervus axis* were very pretty looking as if an Australian aborigine had painted their coats. We were told the males often decorate their antlers with vegetation in the hope that it will attract more females to their herd. With binoculars, we were able to see Golden jackals (*Canis aureus*), water buffalos (*Bubalus bubalis*), and Mugger Crocodiles (*Crocodylus palustis*) shared the same expanse of water. Did the Crocodiles ever take a baby Buffalo, we asked. The guide was not sure but thought not. Water Buffalo are not as peaceful as they look and probably take the life of more humans than the feared Crocodile. A list of birds we saw including many water birds would be too long to describe, a bird watcher's delight. In all, after giving up on seeing a leopard, it was all we expected. We stopped at a bay on the sea's edge to give the driver a rest. The tsunami had entered the park at this spot and destroyed the building that was there, and thirty people died. "Was there any loss of life of the animal population?" They thought not; animals have a fine sense of danger which outstrips all our technology in depicting when a natural disturbance might appear. We humans, who surely once had this instinct but lost it, could do well in observing animals and birds when they act out of character.

Back at Vikum Lodge, we decided to stay another night. Soon after our return, the owner knocked on our door asking if we'd mind paying for the room and yesterday's meals and beer. We did not mind, feeling sorry that this peaceful place had no other guests, leaving the owner with little to do. After a short rest, we were off again to see what there was to be seen. We walked again to the tank and then continued on to Yatala Whera dagoda. Now over two thousand years old, it has had most of its treasures unearthed and put in the museum. We had read about this museum; it was free and sounded interesting, with a bidet with a proper water system and with ugly faces carved around its base with the intention of stopping the user thinking about sex. For some reason, after seeing the dagoda, we moved on, forgetting to visit the museum. This we put down to the fact that on the way, we had seen a whole troop of langur monkeys in the trees when we stopped to have a water coconut. Fascinating to watch, we had lingered but were now keen to return to see if they were still there. They were, but had moved further along to a picnic site. Now we saw they were joined by just one female Toque monkey, who, though smaller, was bossing the langurs who were now sitting in a happy group having a picnic on the leftover food tossed on the ground by humans. Crows and dogs were also competing for all this free food. When a cow joined in, a man shouted and forced her to keep walking. Most of the leftovers had been tossed away wrapped in plastic consumed in quantities could finally kill any animal. There were garbage containers, and they had a lid, a lid that the monkeys were quite capable of lifting. If only people could put their plastic in a bin, or better still take it home and lay out the uneaten food for their distant relations to consume without danger. I was beginning to feel that the people, monks included, did not have the true feelings for others not of their species. True, they would not kill or harm them, but it did not go much further than that.

Here, people were more used to visitors whose interest lay in the local wildlife. A man stopped us and suggested we turn off into a field near the end of the lake where flying dogs hang out. "Flying dogs," we echoed, somewhat in disbelief. As we said it, we at once realised he meant fruit bats, so often called flying foxes. We are both familiar with these bats but took the recommended route and saw them all hanging like odd fruits or black plastic bags on the one tree they had decided was the best.

"Look where you are walking," called Michael. Too late, I had put my foot in a wet muddy patch that did not smell like lavender.

Back at our lodge, well pleased with our day but tired, we had a much-appreciated watermelon, watched by a dog feeding a cute puppy.

At dinner that night, we found we were no longer the only guests. A Belgian couple had arrived. Like us, they wished to visit the park and wanted to share to save expenses. We would have loved to have visited it again and perhaps seen a leopard but felt we could not afford to.

Budurwagala, 15m high Buddha

Beautiful moth

Train ride

Pond turtle

Danger on the new highway

Chapter Six

Views and Tea in the Hill Country

We had arrived in Wellawaya by bus. Booking into a place called 'Little Rose', we wanted to see the figures of Buddha carved into the rock at nearby Buduruwagala; taking a Tuk-tuk to the rock. The central figure of the seven carved into the rock towered above us. We were not surprised it is the tallest in Sri Lanka at 15m. The carvings are thought to date from the tenth century. Figures alone do not impress us, but the workmanship of these carvings did. Was it the work of many artists and how long did it take? Questions no one is able to answer. As a streak of orange on the central figure is still visible, it is thought that at one time they were all brightly coloured. Quite possible, but personally, I prefer to see the natural rock. Michael had me stand in front of the carvings to better gauge the height when he took a photo. There was something about these figures that enthralled me. If I lived nearby, I said I would often come and visit. Michael said I would soon just accept their existence as they became familiar.

Back at the hotel, we had gone for a walk and on our return noticed two large billboards, proclaiming the delight of "Little Rose". They boasted a swimming pool and a picture of a grand building, which bore no resemblance to the place we were staying at. I asked the owner if there was a swimming pool. "Not yet, but in the future," he replied. He was obviously a man who lived in his make-believe future. I thought the best part of the place was the showers. Two shower heads, one slightly higher than the other. I stood between them and got blasted clean. I was very impressed.

The whole area in front of the dining room was full of parked vans and trucks, yet the dining room was empty. Michael asked for a beer; he was in luck they had just the one bottle. We were then asked if we wished to have our dinner there in the dining room. Seeing no other place that would be suitable to eat in, we said yes. We were told that the place was full, all but one room taken. If so, the other guests were exceedingly quiet. The dining room was an odd mixture, with a corrugated tin roof and ceiling, tables covered in plastic, and display cabinets full of very ordinary glasses and china. At one end of the room were three sinks. Not for customers to wash their hands, dirty dishes were waiting to be washed. Along one wall were red fringed curtains to give the place a bit of grandeur. "What," Michael whispered. "Do you suppose is hidden behind the drapes?" "Graves of all the customers who came by the trucks outside and were poisoned," I replied. "As we had come by foot, we decided we would be quite safe.

We were served plenty of food, finding it far too much. We both left a considerable amount, which was moved to another table and covered with newspaper. Halfway through our meal, two local men came and sat at another table eating and not uttering a word. I started to get the feeling I was in a dream. We appreciated our big airy room, but one of the mosquito nets had plastic on the top. It felt as if I had a jellyfish above my bed. There was a cross-stitch picture on the wall. I think it was well done but was a little hard to see; it was quite small but was hung almost as high as the ceiling. Perhaps they were afraid a guest might fancy it and take it away. Funny place, part family home, part truckers pull in, and part hotel, certainly interesting.

Next morning, all the trucks and van were still in place as we called a Tuk-tuk and made for the bus stand. Luck was with us. An empty bus stood waiting. We had the best seats up front, giving us a wide view and Michael plenty of leg room. A beautiful ride going up into the hill country to Ella: winding roads, clear views, hills, and a waterfall.

We had intended to book into the Beauty Mount Tourist Inn. Puff, pant, stop, deep breaths. I barely made it to reception after climbing innumerable steps. Michael continued to check it out, returned saying there were a lot more steps which I would not be able to manage. It's times like these that are really upsetting, finding we are unable to go to certain places because I get too out of breath and my legs refuse to go up hills and steps. This puts paid to long hikes in high places, both of which I love. Friends earlier had suggested Hill Top Guest House, but the very name ruled that out. All the guest houses were set high, no doubt with wonderful views but unobtainable to me. We settled on Dream Café, a room level with the road.

Ella was one place, after reading about it, that we had considered looking at houses for rent. It was all it was reported to be but too high for me to breathe. Finding out that I must have left the food we bought before leaving in the morning on the bus, I gave myself zero marks for not doing very well. We were grateful to find a woman who made fresh juice and agreed to make us a veg curry that night.

We caught a bus to Bandarawela to visit the Dowa Temple. Landed up in the town and had to go back the way we had come by Tuk-tuk. The driver was friendly and he came round with us. Another Buddha cut into the rock not as large as the one we had seen at Buduruwagala but very serene. Looking at it, you felt you could somehow communicate, perhaps due to the thin air I was imagining it. Still feeling enchanted, we went into the huge cave, covered with wonderful murals. I was a bit taken aback to find more steps going up and down but not to be put off, I made my way round. At one point, the driver who entered the caves with us pushed me forward just as I had stepped back to take a photo. This was surprising and a bit uncalled for, in the least I felt, until I turned and saw a cobra was coming through the window behind me. The cobra was on the way back out by the time I saw it. Snakes are nice, and I went to touch the tail, panic from both driver and monk, who then got a stick to close the shutter. Cobras were depicted in the murals so it was quite reasonable to expect a live one to enjoy the cave too.

That night, we enjoyed our rice and curry in the company of an Irish man who worked in Malaysia. He had been delighted with all the surrounding walks. I envied him for his ability, but he was only 33, less than half Michael's age and much younger than yours truly. Back at our café, we decided to splurge and had an Espresso each. The menu was out of date, the machine broken. We settled for filter coffee in huge cups. It was a big disappointment and cost more than our meal. It was also blamed for us not sleeping very well that night.

Rowena Ella Falls, we had a glimpse from the bus on the way to Ella. The whole area is beautiful and was easy to get a bus to from Ella. It was also not spoiled by coach loads of tourists, as we had feared. There were several stalls selling corn and mangoes. Toque monkeys had a good set up, lovely trees, wonderful views, and plenty of water, and of course, they patronised the food stalls. A man approached us, asking for English coins for his son. Not having any, we could not oblige. Before we left, another man approached; this one had three English pound coins and asked us to change them. We gave him Rs. 500, which made him happy but fully expected it to be a scam. One getting coins which the other changes for Rupees, quite enterprising. The only surprise was that the first man did not approach us again to get them back.

Returning to Ella, we checked out the little railway station that was being repainted. Just before we reached it, we were admiring a very colourful garden full of flowering plants. The owner spotted us and our interest, and we were invited in and shown around. His English was good, but he did not know all the English names of the flowers, so was pleased I was able to tell him. They were the same flowers grown in Europe, not tropical, owing to the much cooler climate in the higher regions. Meeting his wife, we were then invited into their home and shown photos. The year before, she had gone to India on a pilgrimage to all the Buddhist sites and taken some very good photos. They were both a very interesting couple and a lucky chance meeting for us.

Back at the "Dream Café", we looked at the back garden. Michael took a photo of a Jambu tree and its fruit. We noticed as we left that a man was putting up a ladder against the tree. A bit later, a bag of fruit was handed to us through the window of our room.

We were leaving the next day and I really wanted to be able to get up to Rawana Holiday Resort, having been told it was vegetarian and the path up to it very near where we stayed. There were steps and then more steps, and the higher we went, the slower I moved. Finally, we arrived, well rewarded by spectacular views. The place was spotless. Ordering a pot of ginger tea, we enjoyed it all the more for its presentation in very nice white china cups. Suddenly, we noticed the rain coming our way and then it tipped down. Until then, we were the only guests. With the rain came a young but amazingly fat girl. "How come she had made it up all those steps without losing weight?" whispered Michael. "I think it's more strange she managed to make it at all," I replied. We looked at the menu. It was not all vegetarian but did have a good-sounding rice and curry. While giving myself a pat on the back for having made it up all the steps, I did not feel it was worth repeating in the evening, in the dark. Coming back down was easy and much shorter than going up.

We met Lani, the jolly Australian/Sri Lankan girl, whom we first met in Marissa and now again in Ella. Upon boarding the train, we reunited with Lani and her friend Sharna. They were going further while we alighted at Haputale. The ride was more than worth the 50p second-class ticket, even though we sat in third class to get a seat. The views were spectacular. I could not help wishing it were possible for me to live in such a place. On the other hand, it was the tropics I wanted to be in.

Leaving the station, we chose the most convenient place to stay. "Royal Top Rest Inn" was very near the station. Feeling extremely tired, I could have quite happily had a sleep. But we only had a one-month visa, and we had already used up 17 days of it. The month we had given ourselves was to find out if Sri Lanka was a place we felt we could happily live in. By then, I think we had enjoyed everything so much and met so many friendly people that we had little doubt that this was the country for us. So instead of taking a nap, we caught a bus to Dambatenne Tea Factory. A tea factory started in the days of colonial rule by the Scot, Sir Thomas Lipton. How often we had noticed the little yellow tags dangling from cups of tea with the name Lipton. Poor Thomas would probably turn in his grave to see tea bags, which surely were not invented when he was around at the end of the nineteenth century. We now passed miles and miles of tea plantations; only at one point did we see women picking the leaves with panniers on their backs. While not unpleasant to look at, all very neat and tidy, it was nevertheless a monocrop. How wonderful it must have looked before the British, with profit in mind, had cut down the jungle and planted coffee. Coffee had been their first enterprise, but when a disease killed the crops, they changed to tea. So tea, to this day, remains. A poor change, I felt, not just because we are not tea drinkers, much preferring coffee, but coffee trees with branches covered in white flowers are so much nicer to see than the small camellia flowers which are all the tea bushes can produce.

Many years before, I had stayed for a day or two with some Scottish tea planters in Darjeeling. From what I remembered, the process of drying the leaves was quite a simple affair. Here, the poor tea leaves go through so many stages of processing, drying, rolling, all done by machine. Then practically toasted and sieved to a fine black dust, which I remembered someone calling the sweeping off the factory floor. Not far wrong as at stages it was laid out on the floor. Now we learn that this dust is considered the best tea. What happened to true tea leaves? How do fortune tellers manage to read tea dust? They showed us various grades, the best are for export. A bit mean leaving the local population with inferior grades. Perhaps it depends on individual taste. Neither of us care for English tea, even when watered down and minus milk and sugar. Here we found the black tea very drinkable. It was all very interesting, and we had a guide take us round and explain the different stages. We did pay and were rather surprised, no free samples or offers to taste the many kinds. It was not organic or Fair Trade. We had passed a Fair Trade outfit but understood the factory we went to was the only one that caters for nosey-parkers. The tea pickers were Tamils, and the surrounds of the factory were decidedly more colourful and interesting. Lines where the pickers lived and the school for the children who at that time were enjoying following us about. We made ourselves more popular by giving them the rest of the Jambu fruit we were carrying. The Hindu temple was by far the most ornate piece of architecture. I always think that it must be such fun to paint all the characters and wonder when they do it as for the most part they look fresh but have yet to see anyone touching them up. Do the Gods do it at night?

We did not go up a higher peak to where Lipton could sit and survey his domain. We were quite high enough and needed to descend.

St Andrew's Church was being decorated for Christmas with a Christmas tree and lots of tinsel. We were not sure we had seen that in a church before. Some of the gravestones and plaques were fun to read; one person drowned by accident, another just died by accident, and a couple of men died on their way back to the UK. We admired the stained-glass window – corrugated iron roof but quite pretty. By now, I was flagging, but Michael was feeling fit and raring to go. A short rest and then off again to visit Adisham Monastery. We walked and walked; I was nearly dropping to sleep on my feet but enjoyed some marvellous views when the mist lifted. I had felt so well at sea level, but My chest, ears, and head all hurt, and I felt so tired. I think we had gone miles when a Tuk-tuk stopped and told us we were too late to see the Monastery as it closed at four, and it was then 30 minutes after. I readily agreed to go with him just to take a look at it. Just as well as we still had some distance to go. On arrival, our driver had rightly summed me up as an old lady that needed support and cut me a stick so I could walk around the edge, managing to see some of the garden and the monastery itself. Very beautiful, lucky old monks.

On our return to our lodging, we found it quite chilly and put on all the clothes we had. We appreciated having hot water in the bathroom. A Frenchman arrived from Tissa. He wore shorts and a tee shirt!

After a very cold night, I said I really did not want to go to a place Michael had picked out, which was even higher and no doubt colder. He agreed, Kandy would be our next stop.

Train in the hill stations

Part of the Hindu temple on the tea estate

Children of Tamil tea coming out of school

Temple of the sacred tooth relic

Chapter Seven

Kandy - Temple of the Tooth

By going to Kandy, we were once again retracing steps we had enjoyed with Pop in 2004.

The trip to Kandy in 2004 was the most enjoyable part of that two-week stay. We had arranged with Sandy to go in his van and stay the night at a hotel. Getting into the van at six in the morning, we were a little alarmed to see six boxes containing our breakfast and lunch. Each box had sliced bread wrapped in cling film, sliced cheese wrapped in cling film. Even the bananas were wrapped in cling film. We suggested that banana leaves and newspaper would have been nicer. No, that was just for the poor people. Sandy was not accompanying us; instead, we had Andre as our guide. Driving inland, we found the roads were better and with less traffic. We passed brilliant green paddy fields, surely the brightest green of any grass, that showed off the white egrets to perfection, who in turn had cows and buffalo as companions, enjoying the ticks and insects that tried to annoy the cattle. This was all new to Pop, who commented on how very different it was from the English countryside.

Our breakfast stop was at a pineapple plantation. Rows and rows of the prickly fellows. Some with the ripening fruit and others more recently planted. A dog was tied to a post, poor thing, and kept barking. All the other dogs we had seen had been free to roam the streets and hold up the traffic if they decided to stop for a scratch. Continuing on our way, we saw another animal with a string round its neck. This time it was a mother porcupine with twins only recently born. It was surprising that under the conditions it lived, held captive and out in the sunshine, it had been able to produce these tiny babies. The Asian porcupine is much smaller than any I had met before. It was sad to see this little family; in the wild, they would be nocturnal and foraging for food. I gave the mother a banana, which she accepted, and was given a quill.

It was obviously a tourist attraction. I asked why the man was allowed to keep them on a lead when it was a wild animal. Never slow with an answer. "To stop them going on the road!"

The elephant orphanage at Pinnewala surprised us with the large number of fully grown elephants to tiny babies, one of which we were invited to touch before being returned to the herd. We had not kept our eyes on Pop and were alarmed to see him mingling with the large elephants. Delighted and unconcerned, unnoticed by anyone, he had got in the centre of the herd who must have sensed his admiration for them and accepted him. He walked out to join us unharmed and quite unaware it was against the rules.

We had hoped to see them getting bathed in the river. According to a notice, it was not bath day. Nearing Kandy, a magnificent view stretched before us. A view devoid of any human structure or life. As if they stepped from the wings of a theatre, two ladies appeared selling spices and necklaces.

We were happy and impressed when we were taken to the hotel Thailanka, our hotel for that night. It occupied a good position, and best of all, troops of Toque monkeys were playing in the grounds and removing tiles from house tops lower down. They reminded me of Singh, my Sri Lankan monkey and travelling companion many years before.

In a travel guide, the same hotel quoted a cost per night a little more than Sandy had charged us for the whole trip with the hotel included. We had requested ground floor rooms, but they apparently did not exist; however, there was a lift which took us out to a perfect view and a walk to steps leading to an artificial rock tunnel. This was a bit dodgy, so Pop accepted a room before the steps. If there were other guests, we did not see them.

Notices on the wall of our rooms warned us to lock the doors to the veranda as the monkeys were quite capable of opening the sliding doors to ransack the rooms. Out on the veranda, we watched the monkeys playing and removing tiles from roofs. I waved a banana in the air, and a monkey started making its way towards me. The monkey was nearly up to me when suddenly the banana was snatched out of my hand by another who had crept up behind me. I allowed the other monkey to groom my hair and would have groomed him back, but oddly he did not wish me to and left.

Pop was also enjoying the place, enthralled by the mountain view, and without him voicing it, we knew he would much rather have spent the holiday with such a view than in Kalutara. He was also smiling at the monkeys. Pop had, at one time in the UK, cared for Singh and built a home for him, complete with a bedroom, so the monkeys brought back happy memories for Pop too.

Rejoicing in the van, we were taken off to see the famous Kandy dancing. We found reserved seats two rows from the front. Michael was not sure he really wanted to see the dancing and Pop remarked that he doubted it would be classical ballet. In the event, we all enjoyed it. The dancing was terrific, and the costumes fantastic. The movements and acrobatics the men did left us breathless. Certainly NOT ballet but most certainly professional. It ended with some fire walking, and the driver came to collect us so he could take us to the temple of the tooth before they closed the road to traffic.

Pop, unlike us, had not rested in the afternoon or eaten very much. Now, he felt tired, and Andre said he felt that the walk about would be too much for Pop as there would be many people. Pop stayed with the driver, and Michael and I joined the crowd visiting the temple of the tooth. It was all quite amazing, and a shame Pop missed it, but he had to agree it would have been too much for him.

I had expected this holy and holistic Buddhist place to be tranquil, a place to contemplate or meditate, where any spoken word would be whispered. We had a very good temple guide who raised his voice to be heard over the loud beating of drums. I had a purple water lily, the Sri Lankan national flower, to give as an offering. The place was packed and included a lot of tourists. Cameras were very much in evidence. An awe-inspiring place, ornate, very oriental, with bright lights and very noisy. A place just to enjoy, even if not really understanding.

At dinner that night, we were all tired, but it had been a day exceeding all our expectations. Pop was up first the next morning, looking cheerful and taking his first photos of the trip, capturing the surrounding mountains. After breakfast, we left at nine to visit a wood carving place. It involved many steps, so only Michael and I visited. Pop would have enjoyed it more as it was much like many we had visited in Thailand and Indonesia.

The Botanical gardens were wonderful, just one thing missing: seats! Pop was enjoying it, but it was a lot of walking and he needed to sit down, so he returned outside with the driver.

The gardens were very well-kept, and the trees all had name labels. When a guide approached us, we were going to tell him we did not need him, preferring to wander around alone. We changed our minds and found him very interesting and knowledgeable. One of the bamboos, whose name I did not record, was a fascinating baby, growing at the rate of 30 cm per day – 3 metres in 3 months. After this spurt of energy, it stops growing when just one and a half years old. A good bamboo to have if you wish for quick results.

The orchids were beautiful, but I found I enjoyed the trees the most and wish we could have stayed longer.

After a couple of hours, we felt we should get back to Pop, imagining him sitting in the minibus. We should not have worried. He was sitting in a chair surrounded by a small crowd of admirers. People were always attracted by his age and smart dressing. He had been given a fizzy drink in a bottle, probably his first fizzy drink ever. He thought it was very nice of them but a funny drink. We turned down the offer of visiting a tea factory and plantation, just stopped for lunch and then back to Kalutara.

Exactly six years and one day after that first journey to Kandy, Michael and I were making the journey by train. I was still feeling tired and ill, and it did not help that our train had standing room only. I was lucky as a man kindly gave me his seat. Michael stood for the next two and a half hours before the one next to me became vacant. The journey was interesting even if we could only enjoy it looking out of the window. Waterfalls and rivers, mountains and paddy fields, acres of tea, then rubber trees, eucalyptus, and palms. The journey seemed longer than we expected. I was feeling so much better it made me realise we had left the hill country behind; the world once more was flat. I could not believe we had missed the station as we had looked out all the time. Michael at first also refused to believe it, putting my return to health down to the fact I was not exerting myself, but I pointed out, just look at the landscape. Neither of us wished to believe we had long passed our station, but it was painfully obvious. So it was not too unexpected when we pulled into Colombo Fort station. Michael raced off to find out the next train back to Kandy; they told him the platform and to hurry. Back down the steps and onto the train just in time. Now retracing our steps but on the other side. As before, we were in the end carriage that always stopped short, so unable to see the names of the stations. Visions of us landing back where we had started that morning. Again we found ourselves standing, but a kind couple, also on the thin side, moved close and let me sit with them. When they alighted, they told us that the train would terminate at Kandy. We breathed a sigh of relief. Our luck was changing. A couple in front had heard our conversation with the people we shared a seat with and turned and said they were also going to Kandy, asking where we were staying. We had decided on "The Pink House". They did not know it but said their house was by the lake, so it would be nearby, and we could go in their car. Our new friends were met in a minibus full of their relatives. They were having a big family reunion.

It was now dark and about eight o'clock. Their house was delightful, and we were invited in but declined the invitation, feeling they would be busy with all their relations. We said we could walk and find "The Pink House". No, they would not think of it, and two men and a young boy got back in the minivan with us and told the driver where to go. Easier said than done, no one knew the way, and it was dark. We did have a phone number, and they had a mobile phone but could get no answer. It was getting embarrassing. We suggested they let us out, and we could take a Tuk-tuk. No, they were determined to find it. Many stops and enquiries and perusal of a map, all the time we were feeling guilty and rather expected that they were looking for something higher class than a simple guest house. Finally, we found it. They were full! Almost next door was another guest house, so we said goodbye to our kind friends and decided we'd stay regardless. The offered room was expensive, well over double the rates at the "Pink House". "Let's live it up; it has been a long day," said Michael.

Once inside, things did not look too good. First, the door would not open; force was applied. When it finally yielded, there was a room half-tiled with dirty bathroom tiles and only one bed. We had stipulated two beds, which we thought they had agreed upon. Now, this was all they had. The room was small and dirty, with a full ashtray placed on a small, dirty table. Perhaps we had mistaken the amount they quoted for one night. Very tired but also hungry, we asked if they had any fruit. There was none and no restaurant. Michael said, "Perhaps we should find another place." The owner heard and brightly said there was hot water in the bathroom. I did not care; we usually preferred cold showers, but by then, I was shaking with fatigue. We agreed to stay, still thinking we must have misunderstood the amount asked for. Michael said he would take a Tuk-tuk and find some fruit, which he did at some expense. Meanwhile, one towel and a sheet were delivered. The bathroom was tiny and flooded when the loo was flushed. The water was cold, and by now, so were we. We tackled the owner again, who appeared very surprised that we wished to shower that night, but said he would put the boiler on. After lukewarm showers we feasted on the fruit Michael had found and soon fell asleep.

Next morning, Michael went to the "Pink House" to see if there was any chance of a room. Yes, someone was leaving. We could have a large room with a bed each; there was a communal area, garden, and we could eat there. How much? Rs. 700 per night. We returned next door to check out. We had not mistaken the rate they charged. Unwillingly, we paid Rs. 1800. The owner was in a wheelchair and perhaps he felt life was not being kind to him and would take it out on other people. Happy to escape such an unwelcoming place, we picked up our packs and moved into the Pink House. In spite of its name, it was much more to our liking. A very friendly place, and we had breakfast with three others staying there who live mainly in India in the Himalayas. It sounded wonderful, if you did not suffer from altitude sickness. When they first started living in India, their visa required them to leave the country once every year. They would then go to Nepal, get their passport stamped, and return if they wished the same day. A change of government or rules and now they have to leave the country each year for two months. They were going to go back to Europe to work. This made us think. By now, we were both enjoying the country so much we had made up our minds to make it our home. As of then, we had not gone into the rules and regulations allowing us to be residents. We had been told the visa was very expensive but living, as we could see, was cheap. If, though, Sri Lanka followed the same rule as India, we might, as we got older, not wish to be away for two months.

Walking round the lake was a treat. It was beautiful, and all the houses and buildings were nice. The best town we had seen. The lake was populated with shags, kingfishers, herons, sitting in the surrounding trees alert to any passing fish. The egrets had nests and fluffy chicks. In the water, monitor lizards swam or lay on the banks, turtles sat on low branches over the water which was so clear we could see fish. In the middle of the lake was an island. Trees lined the shore with monkeys chattering and swinging about trying to get our attention. All the trees have their names clearly marked making it easy to identify them. Reaching the Temple of the Tooth, we watched streams of people heading for the temple, local Buddhists buying flowers at the stalls. The entrances had security booths. Women going in one entrance, men the other, rejoining once through, after being frisked. No doubt necessary in this world today but sad. We had found the perfect place had it not been for my inability to breathe. I had not remembered being affected on our first visit but just walking round the lake on the flat, I was worn out. Visiting a local handicraft centre, we watched a man beating out elephants on thin pieces of brass sheet. I asked for a monkey to add to my collection. It was not as realistic as the elephant. The building was the same one we had seen the dancing with Pop. Now little preschool children were on the stage being tutored in dancing and doing remarkably well for such small ones. We were looking at some paintings and batiks, not for long, as a very persistent man tried to make a sale.

Seats were provided on the edge of the lake, so we bought some food from a stall and sat eating while enjoying the wildlife on the lake. I remained there when Michael went on and met the three from "Pink House." They too had a piece of brass with an elephant picked out. Meanwhile, I was joined by some school boys with excellent English. They were in higher education, which apparently lasted until they were 22 years old. Presumably, they were being supported by their parents until then. They were extremely polite, and one invited me to his home for dinner. A kind offer, but I had to refuse when he told me his home was high above the lake.

Back at the "Pink House", we chatted with the daughter of Eve, our host. She told us her husband was arriving that night and would know of places for rent at sea level. Others told us of nice houses to rent inland from Unawatuna and Hikkaduwa. I was still feeling unwell; a German girl told me to have garlic soup. I asked Eve if she could make me the soup. She had already made me vegetable soup but said she would get garlic. Eight of us sat down to dinner: 1 Austrian, 3 French, and 4 English. It was a nice and jolly meal. Everyone had brought beer. Michael was amazed his was larger and not Stout, but David, one of the three from India, had noticed that is what he had bought.

My soup came with a saucer full of big, juicy garlic cloves. Some I put in the soup and ate the rest. The night had been cold, but I slept until 6:30 and woke feeling much better. Not sure if

I was acclimatizing or if it was the soup and garlic that did the trick. After breakfast, we walked into town. A market full of plants, flowering shrubs, cacti, and even the familiar Michaelmas daisy and goldenrod. The most amazing thing was to see a warehouse full of Noritake china. I was unaware it was still being made. The cloth section of the market sold everything from mosquito netting and sheets to clothes. It was a Poya day, full moon, so I was surprised so much was open. The banks, however, were not. A man tagged onto us, telling us he knew one that was open. It was a money exchange with a lower rate; we declined. We had traveller's cheques, and the man now suggested we go to a jewellery shop, buy something, and they would take a cheque and give us change. We were sure this would have worked but had no desire to buy any kind of jewellery; rather, we would wait until the next day. The man gave up on us and left. Starting to retrace our steps, we were joined by another man, a school teacher this time, who Michael had met before. He told us he was related to Eve, the smiling lady that owned the "Pink House". He was pleasant enough, but we would have preferred to wander at leisure. Obeying orders from our teacher friend, we went to a shopping mall where there was a bank branch that was open, and we quickly changed our traveller's cheques. We had found before a place called Liquid for Life, a slightly odd name but wonderful for fresh fruits and drinks. We told him that was where we were now headed and had been before. He came too, and of course, we felt we had to buy him a fruit salad. He then wanted to show us an open-air church. Not having heard of this, which sounded rather nice, we stupidly agreed. He said it was not far, then told us to stay put and went and got a Tuk-tuk. It was not far; we could easily have walked. We stopped outside some gates leading to a forest. We read that it cost Rs. 500 for each entrance fee. The Tuk-tuk wanted Rs. 180. We settled for Rs. 150 and walked to the closed gate. The teacher friend is now busy having a long chat on his mobile phone. The end result is we are not allowed in. The Tuk-tuk driver, who probably knew this would happen, was still waiting. We got back in and were dropped off more or less where we started with Rs. 200. We said goodbye to the teacher and, looking back, saw that he went back in the Tuk-tuk. We had wasted time and a little money. Back in the shopping mall, we were very happy to find a bookshop which had a good stock of books in English at a very reasonable cost according to the printed price on the back cover. We changed our minds when, about to buy, we were told the price was a lot higher. The printed price referred to Indian rupees.

Devon Restaurant. The name caught our eye. Devon was where we lived in England. The menu outside sounded good and inexpensive, but neither of us was hungry. They did, however, have ginger tea which was enough to entice us in. It was a grand place and full of local people. We were impressed and enjoyed our tea. Returning to our lodging along the lakeside, we met a huge water monitor which we estimated was seven or eight feet long. We also happened to bump into our teacher friend. He told us he had taken lunch and was full. We were pleased to hear this and went our separate ways.

While I enjoyed myself washing clothes in the garden, Michael went out to try to get beer and to see if he could discover where the hotel was that we had stayed in with Pop. No one knew of it, and it was a large place as we remembered. The tourist board tried to be helpful but again drew a blank. On another trip to Kandy that we made a few years later, we clearly saw, up from the lake, the hotel and its name. Michael was unable to get any beer as it was Poya. The ever-resourceful Eve had also tried and failed. Poya days were strictly non-alcoholic.

A new visitor arrived and was given a room opposite ours. Michael had to make her bed after we heard a shout of surprise. The mattress was balanced somehow on the frame. When she sat on it, she landed on the floor. All the wooden slats were missing. On inspection, the missing slats were found on the floor under the bed. The upkeep of the once family home could have been a little better, but any inconvenience mattered little against the very friendly atmosphere. Eve was always all smiles and made us feel she really enjoyed looking after her guests. We enjoyed hearing the experiences of the other guests. We envied the two English men and the Austrian girl their life in the mountains at 2,000 meters. The views sounded idyllic, but I would not be asking for an invite.

We left the next morning with directions on how to find a house that was for rent in Unawatuna. First, though, we would go north to Anuradhapura, a name that rolled pleasantly off the tongue, and my memories going back to 1959 of jungle, and being given Singh, the toque monkey.

Life on Kandy Lake

Chapter Eight

Anuradapura

Leaving Kandy by bus, we managed to get seats together. We saw a lot of the town and very nice houses in grounds set back from the road. After that, rain fell down, blocking out any view and finding its way into the bus even with all windows closed. We would probably have been better off outside with an umbrella.

Arriving at Anuradapura bus station, we found a Tuk-tuk that took us to the "Lake View Guest House". A charming man greeted us and gave us a super clean room with towels, etc. This was not the Anuradapura I remembered. The town was huge. Perhaps it was a mistake coming back. I was not quite sure what it was that I hoped to recapture.

In 1959, after my boyfriend and I arrived from India to Ceylon, we must have got a lift to the modern town of Anuradapura as we were hitchhiking. However, all memory of that has been erased from my brain. We were very ignorant then of the history of many places we visited, which only added to the wonder of travel. Everything we saw was a revelation. We discovered places regardless that millions had seen it all before. With no expectations, we were never disappointed. My memory starts when we bumped into an Englishman working in the country. He suggested we go for a beer. We declined at first, knowing that beer is expensive and we only ever spent on necessaries. Perhaps he guessed from our appearance why we refused, so added it would be his treat. It certainly was a treat for us. He was travelling inland the following day, into the jungle to service an organ for some Catholics. What a strange thing to do, we thought, but when asked if we would like me to accompany him, we jumped at the chance. In conversations, he knew I loved monkeys and he promised we would be able to see a lot. I pictured thick jungle with a small clearing in which a man sat at an organ, belting out hymns to an audience of monkeys and other wildlife peeping down from the trees.

The next day found us in a small village in which there was a Catholic school for boys. Here we were left with two priests, our friend having disappeared to do whatever he had to do to the organ. Chatting to these men of the cloth, we learned a lot about the surrounding vegetation. For the first time, we ate cooked plantain. They told us the difference between the big green plantains for cooking and the sweet bananas we were familiar with. The boys milled around joining in; most, if not all, spoke English.

Peace was suddenly broken when our friend reappeared with a tiny screaming monkey with a string around its waist. We had not seen the promised monkeys and now I was horrified. The poor little monkey was frightened and trying to get away but held at a distance so it could not bite. Our friend was only too glad to thrust the poor monkey into my arms where it at once stopped its screaming, hanging on tight to me. Where had he got it? "Bought it off some kids in the village," he said. "Does it not have a mother?" I enquired. "No, there is no mother." I suppose I should have been grateful that he had bought me a monkey, but I wanted to see monkeys in the wild and had not anticipated adopting one.

I walked with what was obviously now my monkey around the trees, in the hope we might see a troop of his relations that would take him back to his mother. None came, and now my little friend was digging in the earth, finding small roots to eat. He was at ease, appearing to have adopted me as his mother.

All the boys at the school were in good health, and the sick bay was empty. We were invited to spend the night there. "What shall we call this monkey?" I asked Don. "Well, he is Singhalese, he should have a local name." "Why not then just call him Singh?" Singh he became; we did not dare ask the Priests to christen him as not sure how Catholics felt about their hairy relations. Just before retiring, Singh surprised me by leaping off my lap and up a tree. What should I do? I love monkeys but believe they should be in the wild. On the other hand, a baby has to be with its mother to learn how to cope. Travelling with a monkey on my back might just create problems. I voiced these conflicting thoughts. I agreed with Don; it was really not up to us anymore, Singh had to decide. I called to him, he just looked down at me as if to say, "This is where I belong."

Next morning, one of the boys asked, "Do you want your monkey back?" There was Singh, still in the same tree but lower than before, the string still around his waist, dangling within reach. I held it lightly, and Singh jumped into my arms. The decision was no longer mine to make.

We were lucky and were given a ride by three young men in a car going to Colombo.

At this point, I am sure many readers will not credit that we did not go and visit the ruins of the city of Anuradhapura, that go back 2,000 years or so. Once the capital with a colourful past. At that time, neither I nor Don had ever heard of them. We must have missed many a famous place in our travels through ignorance, but what you don't know you do not miss. We always had the joy of finding places that to us were unheard of.

Returning to our visit in 2010, Michael and I were, of course, well aware of the existence of the ruins and were looking forward to seeing them. It would have been hopeless trying to find that Catholic boys' school in the jungle, where a little monkey named Singh became part of my life. In all likelihood, it no longer was there; the jungle could have taken over, or it may have expanded and now be a city. Either way, I would not recognise it.

The rain still tipped down. I had a packer Mac and Michael had an umbrella, thus armed we walked to the sacred Bodhi tree – Sri Maha Bodhi. This large tree is reputed to have started life as a cutting from Bodhgaya. I had, with Don, seen the parent of this sacred tree in India. Yet now I felt it was not the same kind, and looking at Sri Maha Bodhi, I felt sure I had seen it before. Memory plays funny tricks sometimes. All this time, the rain fell down, and we were wet to our skins. Very few people about which was not too surprising considering the weather. Monkeys were there in numbers. Twice we were approached by men saying they were poor and hungry; they did not look it and had more flesh on their bodies than we did. We suspected they were the kind we had been told about that would take money offered and buy drink with it. Considering this was such an important religious site, it was a shame that it was considered necessary to frisk people who were visiting; many of them were genuine pilgrims. As in Kandy, men and women were frisked by their own sex. Strangely, they did not bother with Michael, but I even had to open my rain jacket and small pack. A female dog attached itself to us; if we stopped, so did she and then followed. She was spotted by a guard when we neared the sacred tree and shooed away. Unfair as other dogs were roaming around. Then we saw an officer or guard with a slingshot, firing at the monkeys. Had people changed or had the empathy I felt before that Sri Lankans had with animals been based on too few cases?

Back in the guest house, we laid out every stitch we had been wearing to dry, plus our money, etc. The weather was kinder to us the following day, overcast but only the odd spot of rain. This allowed us to visit all the historic sights, starting with Tsurumuniya Vihara, a rock temple over two thousand years old. We found this a tranquil place, which is not always the case here. At the altar, some flowers had been placed and a bottle of lamp oil. We watched with amusement when a palm squirrel arrived and set to, eating the flowers. When that was done, it tried to unscrew the top of the lamp oil. It failed to remove it and went off, no doubt to see what other mischief it could get up to. We went to the museum to see most of the carvings which have been removed from the rock temple. We were pleased to see some elephants had been left in place, and outside we made out the figure of a horse. One cave had a rock entrance with carved birds and 3 monkeys. Our attention was then taken by a beautiful black butterfly with the edges of its wings picked out in white. We climbed the rock to find a cave with a reclining Buddha, frescoes on the walls and ceiling. Another cave had been taken over by swallows. A large tarpaulin had been placed on the ground to catch the droppings. A crack in the wall was packed tight with very communal bats. One Dagoba was being restored, with no sign of any workmen; just piles of wood, bricks, etc., indicating restoration was being thought about. The archaeological museum, which we sadly decided to miss, was asking for US$25 a ticket. Time passed as we explored all the ruins, and after seven hours, we felt it was time to return to our lodgings. We would have liked to have stayed longer, but our time was running short, and we wanted to see the houses for rent we had been told about in the south. We saw some lovely houses in Anuradhapura, but no one around to talk to. While we had got soaked to the skin, we knew it could be very dry and hot in that area. Being keen gardeners, we preferred to be in the wet zone.

Chapter Nine

Christmas in Negombo

We left just after seven the next morning, having decided to take a bus to Negombo. Luck was with us as a driver of a mini bus gave us a free lift to the bus station. The first bus that came was going our way, but it was very crowded and we had a long drive ahead of us. Instead of taking it, we bought some veg. Roti and watched the monkeys, once again scrounging in the garbage. We tossed one an orange, but he was too slow and it rolled down a slope. He did not bother to go after it; there were easier pickings in the garbage.

Our bus came in empty, and we got our preferred seats up front. Michael spoke to what he believed to be the driver who told us we would be on the road by eight. We expected to be going when the driver returned, but there were important things to be done to the bus before we could take off, such as redecorating it. The front of the bus already had artificial flowers, but from a large bag, the driver extracted more to add to them and was very careful how he arranged them. He then pulled out five Buddhist pictures and a new tube of glue; the glue gave him a lot of trouble. We watched, too interested to offer help. Finally, he managed to get the glue flowing when he found a toothpick in the upholstery. With a bit of help from the conductor, all five pictures now brightened the front of the bus. Music was turned on, and five sticks of incense lit. Satisfied with the result, the driver leaves the bus, it is now eight-thirty. A lot more passengers had by then joined the bus and kept getting on and off. A bus going our way takes off. We have already paid so compelled to sit in hope of moving. Michael gets off and asks once again when we leave. This time told nine-ten, nearly two hours from when we had got on the bus. We notice the sign on the bus, "Semi Luxury Service". The conductor gets in the driving seat and the engine is warming up. With much horn blowing, we set off. The driver busy talking on the phone he was handed. It did not get far when we had a ten-minute stop so we can stretch our legs, in reality to allow more passengers to board. The bus now fully loaded with people standing, closely packed. The driver, now back in the driving seat and driving relatively slowly, compared with the fast crazy driving we were getting used to. Nearing our destination, he went mad, going at top speed. We thought we were going to the bus station but were told to get off at a minor road.

A Tuk-tuk took us to Beach Villa Guest House where we had a small room with two beds and a shower, but no loo. We were on a wide beach. It was the 23rd of December, and it was very clear that Negombo, unlike other places we had visited, was a Christian town. We did not walk far to find a pink Catholic church. Inside, we saw a decorated tree, actually part of a casuarina tree, and a nativity scene was being erected. Before entering the town, we had noticed stalls with rather gross blow-up Father Christmases and casuarina tree branches being used as Christmas trees. A point in their favour, only now, two days before Christmas, were they starting to decorate, not a month or so in advance. When on becomes sick and tired of it all before the day. Later, the rain came and cleared the beaches. While walking around, we passed restaurants; most had similar menus, not cheap and not very Sri Lankan, with nearly all meat and seafood dishes. We could smell the souvenir shops, which were mainly full of what we considered awful leather goods. No monkeys or much wildlife around. Along the beach, several big hotels looked like package tourists; people were spread out on loungers in swimwear, expecting the sun. Rather disappointing for them, it rained. We returned to our guest house, suddenly very tired, and we both fell asleep. The rain persisted, so we stayed put, reading magazines and books in the communal dining room. A man wandered in with no shirt and no teeth. I said he looked drunk. Michael said he had probably been gambling and lost his shirt and teeth. As he went back out, two very gross Chinese girls came in clutching a newspaper bag of food and a bottle of ketchup, with which they liberally shook over the food. Nice place, but not very jolly. The following day we explored for six hours. First, the fishing harbour, hundreds of boats, very picturesque. Spread over the sand to dry were what must have amounted to thousands, if not millions, of dead fish, of different kinds. A man attached himself to us, telling us he had been in a movie made by westerners. He had taken part by explaining about the fishing. He picked up the head of some poor fish. It was very hard, like leather.

The crows and seagulls were, to our minds, acting rather strangely. They were busy fighting over one pile of fish while ignoring all the others spread out to dry. We discovered the ignored fish had been salted, and birds do not like their fish salted. All the fishermen were Catholic, and the harbour was protected by a large figure of the patron saint of fishing. We got a little tired of people asking us for school pens, bonbons, and money. In some cases, it seemed more like a demand to which we did not comply. We went down some small streets with nice little local houses, and here the children and adults were smiling and friendly, not demanding.

Churches and more churches, we lost count of the number we had seen. Here, instead of glass display boxes on the street containing Buddha, they had the Virgin Mary. We visited one or two churches. A few young boys were practising in one, walking between the pews, the leader swinging incense. Two holding crosses and two with bells, two more walked behind with nothing to do, perhaps stand-ins. All the churches were being decorated for the morrow, Christmas Day. All had mangers which were still empty, only one or two having a few chipped plaster animals in. Empty small mangers were being sold along with some brightly painted plaster nativity figures. We found ourselves at the "The New Rest House". It had an air of dignified decay about it. A Government rest house from a bygone era. The first and only of its kind we had found. These rest houses were once dotted all over the country according to the old books of travellers' tales, and we would have loved to have them back. This one claimed the privilege of hosting a visit in 1958 of Queen Elizabeth. Now it is a mixture of grandeur, with some elegant local furniture and a really beautiful stairway. Along with the most awful wood-painted chairs all chipped and tables covered in oilcloth. We had a beer while sitting in planter's chairs, served in nice glasses. Asking how much it cost to stay, told Rs. 1500, they only had two rooms occupied at present by locals. We were rather tempted to stay, but it hardly seemed worth it for one night. Also, it was not a place to meet other people.

At the station, we asked the times of the trains, intending to leave on the 26th. In the residential areas, we had seen some very nice houses, but we were not feeling so comfortable in these surroundings as we had been in areas predominantly Buddhist. By now, we had enjoyed Sri Lanka so much that there was no doubt in our minds that we wished to make it our home. The climate and the people of the southwest appealed to us the most. It was time to find a house we liked and put our house in Devon on the market.

We had originally intended to stay on Christmas day, but by the morning, we knew we could not stand another day. First, we had been unable to sleep due to very loud music on the beach, which certainly was not carols. This went on until after midnight. Worse was to come - firecrackers! If we had not known better, we would have thought we were in a war zone and under fire. Bang after bang sounded as if all were at our wall separating us from the beach.

"Merry Christmas!" we called to each other over the noise. I then found under my pillow a card. A picture of Father Christmas on an island with a palm tree and a monkey. Inside, I read, "Hope you find our monkey island and spend many hot and sunny days in the warm. Love, Hargreaves," from my brother Michael, for whom I had nothing.

When we checked out, the owner said we were lucky all the firecrackers used to start on the first of December, ten years ago. Asking why they did it, we were told the fishermen were sending messages to God. We never got the fishermen's side of the story but did wonder what happened to Peace on Earth. After paying a very reasonable bill, we caught a Tuk-tuk to the station. There was a large nativity display at the station now, and all the others we passed on the way had their full complement of Jesus, Mary, and the animals.

Chapter Ten

The Last Five Days

Christmas Day was spent on the long train ride back south. We arrived at Colombo Fort station around noon and left for Galle two hours later,

The welcoming family at Beach Haven was surprised to see us a day earlier than expected. They were full but provided us with a perfect space for the night. I on a couch and Michael on a camp bed, all free of charge. Already we felt we were among friends, not realizing what a very deep friendship it would turn out to be several years ahead.

We met Ray from the UK, a lone traveller who was at Beach Haven for the second time. Ray joined us for a beer before we all went out to the Indian Hut for dinner. Christmas crackers and the train journey were forgotten.

The next day was most enjoyable, and the first time we did anything constructive regarding finding a future home. Ray joined us as we set out to find the house in Unawatuna we had been told about in Kandy. The first Tuk-tuk we approached knew the house we were looking for, Peru House. He told us it belonged to an Italian; odd, we thought it was owned by a local man. Not to worry, it had to be the same place. Our driver told us that inside the house, it was very interesting with old things. He had been in it for some reason, to do with taking photos. This all sounded promising. Both Ray and the driver had mobile phones and tried phoning the number we had been given. No reply. We decided to go anyway to see where it was. We liked the position and large garden with an old house set back but obscured from view. The gate was locked, the neighbours said no one was at home.

Our driver now said he had a house for rent, and we agreed to take a look at it. The road¾if it could be called that¾was a very bumpy track. The house was interesting, but his parents were living in it. The driver had his own house nearby. We could not understand where his parents would go if we rented it. The house would need some work done on it, but the big drawback was when we realised we had seen all there was to see but not any kind of bathroom. On asking, the owner pointed at a wee shack a little distance from the house. We rather think it served both his house and his parents. On inspection, it had a squat loo with a shower above. OK for a short stay, but we wished for something a bit more upmarket. The ground surrounding the house was large, but we voiced our fear that it might be built on in the future. He informed us he owned all the land and so no one could build on it. We all had the same unspoken thought. Nothing would stop him from building on it. He was friendly, also a good salesman, pointing out he would be nearby, so if anything needed doing he would be there and also we could use his Tuk-tuk. The rent he asked for worked out at about £355 per month. The deciding factor was when he asked for five years' rent in advance. We were not prepared to pay that.

Back on the beach, over a beer and a nice but very expensive espresso coffee, we all agreed that the house had not been for rent until the driver decided he could be on to a good thing, learning we were looking for a place.

The other place we had been told of was at the other end of the beach. Near B's Place was another beach with families of locals really enjoying splashing about in the sea, in contrast to bored-looking tourists on loungers on the rest of the beach. We had been told to ask for the Bay Hotel, which we did, but no one knew of it until as we were walking away, someone came up and told us to cross a little bridge, which we had tried but turned back too soon. We tried again and found a notice on a gate saying "House to Rent." It was already rented, and they were looking for short holiday rents. The next one, proclaiming it was for rent, was wide open, windows and doors, but not a soul in sight or hearing distance. We walked around the garden, calling, to no avail.

Continuing on, we came across by far the best place we had seen that morning. However, this said "FOR SALE". We stood gaping at it when Dieter, the owner, appeared and invited us in. Dieter originally came from Germany; he was a Buddhist artist and had been living there for many years. The place was all one could wish for: a big patio going round the house, a spacious living area, and wonderful double beds, etc. He had not thought of renting, and the amount he wanted to sell for would have been way out of our reach if and when we sold our house in the UK. At our age, to buy we felt would not be a wise decision. After seeing Dieter's place, we feared other places would not appear so nice. Returning along the road, we met a man we had met and talked to before. He had a house, but that also was for sale, but he said he would consider renting it. Strange that if we mentioned we were looking for a house, everyone found they had one for sale or rent. We called into B's place, but Brian was out.

It had been quite an exciting day, and at least we had made a start. Ray said he had enjoyed coming around with us and suggested we should ask more questions when inquiring about a house to rent. This was useful and something to remember when we came again to house hunt, as we fully intended.

More house hunting the next day, our last in Galle. Julie, an artist from Dorset, offered to drive us to see a couple of places near Galle. The first house we quickly crossed off our list. In the sound of traffic and half occupied by the owner and not much of a garden. The next was better in some ways, but it was still in the process of being built. The garden was not large and covered in building materials. Also, as they pointed out, near town. This, for most people, would be an advantage, but we preferred to distance ourselves from any town.

That evening, Michael and I went to a puppet workshop only to find it had finished, but there was a show of very large puppets which was fun. Ray came along with Julie. For the last time on that trip, we ate at the Indian Hut. The next day we would head back to Negombo before leaving, hoping that things were back to normal with no firecrackers.

As usual at Beach Haven, we enjoyed a very good breakfast and were given bananas to take with us. I thought we were packed and ready to go, but Michael said he was sure he had not packed his shaver or battery charger. We tipped everything out of his pack, which was the only possible place these items could be. "I told you I had not packed them; they have just vanished," Michael said as he pushed everything back into his pack. It was obvious that they were not in the room, but I did not believe in objects just vanishing. I pulled back the curtains to shed more light in the room; both items were on the windowsill.

We joined Ray, and the three of us managed to squeeze into a Tuk-tuk. Ray was no lightweight, and his pack was huge, but the station was not far.

The train came in an hour before it departed. This was good news as we were able to get seats together. Alighting at Colombo Fort, Michael and I were about to climb the steps to the next platform. Ray had a better idea; copied from watching the locals, we just crossed the rails to the platform. Sometime later, we were back in our old room in Negombo.

While we shared a beer, an English woman came in that Ray had met before. Chris from Bishops Stratford. She joined us, and two Dutch girls we had met in Galle arrived. This time, a nice party. Michael had developed a bad cold and went to bed, only managing to get up to have dinner with Ray, Chris, and myself. We were all leaving on the 30th. Ray very early to catch a plane to Dubai and meet his girlfriend before returning to the UK. Chris was off to India, and we to Bangkok. We had just one more day in Negombo.

Next morning, the four of us set out. Now, all the empty cribs we had seen before had their brightly coloured figures in place. We walked past the drying fish and were spotted by the same man who had related his movie role to us the week before. He wanted to repeat his story, which must have been the highlight of his life. It was nice that he enjoyed it so. We felt the other two must experience "The New Guest House" where we sat and had a beer in style.

We then arranged transport to the airport. Ray would leave late that night, and Chris would be with us at five the following morning. Chris was fun and quite a character. We learned that she had looked after her mother all her life. Her mother passed away, and Chris, now a pensioner, decided to travel – a brave and wonderful idea on her part. Once, when told the price for something, she looked shocked and said, "That is more than my pension." We found a Tuk-tuk that was willing to take us to the airport early the next morning and agreed on a price. Chris waggled her finger at him and told him to be sure not to oversleep and to arrive on time. He agreed, smiling.

Having a last drink with Ray that evening after Chris went off to bed, we were startled to hear a loud frightened scream coming from Chris's room. We jumped up, as did a number of the staff, to be greeted by a very upset Chris. She had gone into the bathroom adjoining her room only to see a very ugly Chinese woman standing there. Had she had a vision? Was it a ghost? We gathered round as Chris exploded. "It was real," she insisted. Naturally, she had thought the bathroom leading from her room was hers and hers alone. She was very funny and volatile. Such an unexpected shock might have killed her. The staff stood round trying not to laugh. What happened to the Chinese woman, we never heard, nor did we ever see her. Perhaps she had gone back to her room and died of shock. We agreed that finding a Chinese woman in your bathroom whom you had not been introduced to was a bit much. Ray treated us all to a drink, and we said our goodbyes and good nights.

The alarm woke us, and the Tuk-tuk came early. Chris was up and now over her shock from last night.

All the streets were lit up with coloured lights on the way to the airport. After paying the driver, agreed amount which Chris had bargained for, she emptied her purse into his hand, saying she no no longer had need of that currency. We said goodbye and then met again in the airport as we kept being told to go to different departure gates. The last we saw of Chris was sitting at one of the departure gates for a delayed plane. We wished her well and hoped she enjoyed many adventures in India.

Goodbye, Sri Lanka, we will be back.

Realizing Our Dream

Water Monitor

Blackie & Rosie liked to sit in the grave of our new home

A nest full of baby fantails

We were to return to Sri Lanka several times during the next few years. One mistake we made was going to an agency that had property for rent. All were way out of our price range for catering to people coming for a holiday. We were given a lot of help and taken to houses for rent by friends, but something was wrong with all of them. We saw huge houses we thought were ugly with little land, small ones with clothes all over the place, and near a very noisy school so we could not hear ourselves speak. Some were perfect in every way but had steps which, while I could puff my way up, I felt would soon become impossible.

By then, we had found out more about getting a resident visa. It would not be cheap, and we would have to show our bank balance. The item that shocked us the most was that we would have to have, each month, the sum of £1,000 credited to our bank in Sri Lanka, and we could not even take out a bank account until we had a visa. The requirements for a couple, consisting of a husband and wife, were £1,000 for the husband and a further £700 for the wife. Subsequently, we discovered that being brother and sister did not count, and we would both have to have a thousand pounds per month. This was called our pension money. I suppose a few people get that amount in the UK, but our joint state pension, the only one we had, amounted to just over £500 per month. This was OK in England, so what in the world could we possibly spend a total of £2,000 each month in Sri Lanka where living was so much cheaper.

We still had the house in Devon that we had put up for sale. It did not help when we were told that if we had put it up for sale a few years before, we would have expected to get more, and it would have sold faster. We were trying to sell when, for some reason, no one wished to buy.

On one visit, we had seen one house we really liked and also met the owner, Henry, who was later to become a good friend. However, we felt the rent was high, not then knowing how much we would have to spend. Naturally, we could not make any firm decision until we sold our UK home. We were having second thoughts. Did we really want to settle in any place? Michael was easy, "It is up to you to decide. I do not mind what we do," Michael would say as we pondered the facts. "One thing is, what do you intend to do with all your books, pictures, etc.?" That, I felt, would be no trouble; we would get them packed and shipped out. I had a very large monkey collection: 80 pictures ranging from antique to modern, hundreds of ornaments, and other useful items that depicted monkeys. That I would find a charity to give it all to. In the event that was not easily done... Privately, I felt I would like to put in store books and treasures collected from my travels, sell the house, and just be free to travel. I knew the reaction to that idea; that I must remember my age, I was getting too old to just wander about. For me, that was like not living.

By now, I had a laptop and could visit the internet. I hunted for places to rent in Sri Lanka. Most of the agencies were for short stays. Three sounded possible and had photos, so I sent off emails. Only one replied; the other two did, but months later. It was an unpretentious house with land and coconut palms. We liked the look of it. We had now decided to go out just one more time, make up our minds if we found a suitable house, and then hope to sell the house. The market, we were told, was looking up.

We set off in November 2013 with a now-or-never attitude. We made straight for Beach Haven and arrived at ten in the morning, dead tired. We fell asleep until the afternoon when we managed to visit the Royal Dutch Café to say hello to Fazal. We ate at the Indian

Hut and retired for the night at seven-thirty. We were looking forward to seeing the one house I had found on the internet. I had emailed the owner for more details, and he had replied but told me about a plot of land on the beach with permission to build a house with a swimming pool. As we did not wish to buy or build, be on the beach, or have a swimming pool, this was not very helpful. I emailed back - what happened to the house in Talpe? The reply informed me that nothing had happened to it; it was still there, and we could contact him when we got to Galle, and he would show it to us. That felt more like it.

Sharomi is always so helpful at Beach Haven. She made a phone call to the owner, whom we will henceforth call LJS, the owner of the house, found on the internet. She spoke to him on our behalf, and it did not sound very hopeful. It turned out it was not his alone to sell but owned by several people, and that the interior was not good, among other very off-putting things. After all that, he agreed to pick us up and show us the house. Sharomi said her husband would show us a house in the evening.

We were collected in a large car. We were having doubts about LJS, but he appeared normal and friendly. The house was just like the photo, along with the coconut palms. What had not shown in the picture was that it was set back but near the main road. And behind was the rail track. The position itself was not what we wanted, and the inside was such a mess it looked as if it needed rebuilding. We judged it had not been touched since the tsunami nine years before.

LJS had also brought along his nephew who now piped up that he knew of another house for rent in Talpe. We turned down a road away from the main road near the station. Over the rail tracks, there appeared the perfect house set in two acres of flat land with just about every type of fruit and spice tree, plus orchids, plus monkeys. This we both felt was just perfect. It was walled with a high gate, and the back boarded onto a river. We fell in love with the land. The house was fine but needed a lot doing to it, and work was in progress. The owner, who spoke to LJS on the phone, said he could get it all shipshape in a month. We said no hurry and we would have to sell our house first. The rent was higher than expected, but if we had so much money coming in each month, that would not be a problem. There were garages with two rooms on top. Amazingly, we had found our dream home!

We were taken to two other places which were not anything like as attractive. We had had our doubts about LJS at first, but he had good English and was now quite charming, showing us around first to Unawatuna, now a popular tourist place with hotels and restaurants right along the beach. Arthur C. Clarke, he told us, was the first European to live in Unawatuna. He, alas, was no more, but the second is still very much alive, and he said he would take us to visit him. We arrived at this man's house; amazingly, we knew him. Dieter, the German man whose house we had been enchanted with three years before, was still there, having, like us, not been able to sell. Dieter, an artist of religious Buddhist painting and a Buddhist himself, was a very interesting man. We enjoyed meeting him once again, LJS had been surprised that we had met Dieter before and not known his claim to fame as the second European to make his home there. Before returning us to Beach Haven, he took us around his toy factory, run like a cottage industry, which was interesting in itself. Later that afternoon, Lalith, Sharomi's husband, showed us a house. We liked the house, but it was off a small street in town with other houses all around, and the garden was small, mostly grass. We felt bad about turning down this house as Lalith and the whole family are so kind and helpful, but explained we had really fallen in love with the house we had seen earlier. The family wanted us to live in town, saying it is safer. Being safe, and from what we do not know, is something we never think about. We rounded off the day by going back to the Royal Dutch Café for some spicy tea, and Fazal gave me a bracelet. The end of a most successful and enjoyable day.

The next morning, I woke feeling very happy and surrounded by friends. Sita gave me a notebook and a huge bag of tea from their tea estate. She explained they were worried about us wanting to live in a remote place and would prefer us to live in town.

The Talpe house that we were so taken with was not settled on as we had not met the owner; all the details were via LJS on the phone. It seemed prudent to continue looking at places. We went to an agency, but they had nothing, and then looked at my notes for a house in Hikkaduwa, then realising it was with the agency we had just visited. Later, we went back to the agency to be told the Hikkaduwa property had been taken. We felt this was an omen that the Talpe property would be ours.

We ate at The Royal Dutch again. Fazal gave us his card and told us to contact him if we needed any kind of help; we were surrounded by kind people. Fazal also wanted us to be in town and said he would show us houses tomorrow. We agreed but still felt we had found our dream home.

Over the next eight days, we lost count of the number of houses we were shown by various people. Asoka, from B's place, took time off to show us three houses; two were huge but very unattractive and, as Asoka said, very overpriced. The third house was the smallest place we had seen. Lalith took us to one after dark, and from what we could see of the garden, it looked perfect but only one bathroom and to get to it had to go through one of the bedrooms, which we felt was not very convenient. Lalith agreed, and we looked to see if another could be built. The owner showed Lalith one outside, and he exclaimed that we could not expect to use that. I felt that we had raised our sights too high but could not get the Talpe house out of our minds. Two of the most attractive houses were gingerbread houses with lacy fretwork. We loved the look, but one was quite extraordinary inside; upstairs, the rooms were hardly visible, being full of wood. They said we would not need to use upstairs, true, but hardly the point, and where would we put any visitors? The other house had very little garden.

We had bought a mobile phone, as we needed to keep in touch with all the people taking us to see property. We hated the idea of having a mobile and decided we would never have one, having read that the masts were killing bees and the Coltan they put inside was being mined illegally in the mountains of Uganda/Rwanda in the areas set aside for wildlife, mainly the wonderful Ape, the Mountain Gorilla. Also, children were told not to use them as they might affect the brain. To other people, we appeared very old-fashioned; we agreed we were but old enough to remember the days when life was so much simpler. Under pressure, we bought a second-hand one; every time it ran out of money, we bought a card and had to get the young daughter of Sharomi to read and put in the number.

Between house hunting, we enjoyed walking around the ramparts of Galle Fort, even more so when we spotted purple-faced monkeys in the trees. A bus ride to Koggala, where we took an interesting boat ride on the lake. Birds were everywhere we went. There was no doubt in our minds that this was the area we wished to live in. Our notebook, Sita, had given us, was filling up with names and places of houses we had seen. Several we had given good reviews, and at one time would have jumped at them, but the Talpe house was the one we both loved best.

We started to get worried when the week passed and still we had not met the owner of the Talpe property and heard nothing more from LJS.

One Saturday night, Sita invited us to a family dinner. We were already feeling like part of the family by then. We ate more than well that night: two kinds of rice, white and red, and countless delicious curries. We surprised ourselves at how much we managed to put away. Then ice cream. Neither of us could remember when we last had ice cream, only that we do not like it, but ate this out of politeness with no ill effects. Going to bed that night, we felt full and very happy.

As word went round that we were in the market for renting a place, more people came up to us telling us of wonderful places they could show us. Some were very surprising. We had been told of a big house with one and a half acres. So, we were rather amazed when we drove up the driveway of what was signposted as the "Palm Hotel". As a hotel, it must have failed, and theowners had given up. They had stripped out everything, bathroom fittings, etc., and left an awful mess. The garden, too, was a disappointment, large yes, but with a lot of concrete foundations. Small buildings which once might have been loos or changing rooms, but like the house had been stripped bare. There were even a few graves. To rent it was cheap, and should have been; it would cost a fortune to make it into anything liveable.

Another was described as having wonderful views. This proved true, and fifty to sixty acres of land. This was far more than we wanted but we were told the owners would harvest the cinnamon, etc. The house was modern and not very attractive. Set on a cliff edge with a large glassed-in viewing point or veranda. The interior was oddly arranged, and the steep walk up to the house was rather off-putting. With so much land given, as is usual to cash crops, there was very little flat space where one could make a garden. Some two or more years later, when we were living in the area, someone took us again to the same house. It must have changed owners and was well decorated in a modern style, and the awful black leather, or was it plastic, couch had gone. The driveway was just as steep, but at the bottom was a lovely lily pond and garden. Still, it was not our type of place.

I mentioned the black leather/plastic couch. This same couch featured in a number of houses we visited. We do not use leather, but even if it were artificial, we thought it was so unsuitable for the tropics. Quite sweaty to sit on, we thought. We like bamboo furniture and caned chairs which are cooler to sit on, but modern European-style furniture is sought after here. The other most noticeable thing was framed photographs of family members, school groups, wedding photos, and photos of the family's children. If any family had pets, we are yet to see their photo added to this display, which in a couple of cases was arranged on the floor in a corner, rather than hung on the wall. Anything else that might come under the heading of a picture is usually bright-coloured Buddhist posters. All Buddhist homes have a small statue or plaque of Buddha with an electric light permanently on, rather like small house shrines seen in homes in Catholic countries. We very rarely saw polished wooden floors. Some floors are tiled with very large tiles or cement coloured and polished to look like stone or marble. This makes them very easy to sweep and wash and cool to walk on. Concerning floors, footwear is not worn in the house but kicked off outside the door. Flip flops are the most usual and easiest to slip on and off.

The size of the house we found most often referred to the number of rooms, but by this, they mean bedrooms. Some of the houses had kitchens within the house, but more often in the older ones, the kitchen was a separate building. Just a step or two from the house proper. To have two kitchens is quite common. One with a gas burner, bottled gas cupboards, sink, etc., the other with a wide-open chimney where cooking is carried out on terracotta wood-burning stands with clay cooking pots. These cooking pots cost very little and are, to my mind, the best way to cook. I have had clay pots for years, and they were, one by one, getting broken or losing their lids. In Sri Lanka, I was able to replace lids and pots as they broke. I love this idea of having a wood-burning kitchen equipped with a coconut grinder, mortar and pestle, and wooden coconut utensils. The thing about the Talpe house was the kitchen was part of the house and at the first viewing had little in it.

We were given a lot of advice. Someone advised us to phone an English lady called Barbara, who is quite well known by many people even if they have not met her personally. She sounded like a wonderful person, happy to advise and help people like us. We were told that she lives in a lovely house with 80 dogs! After training as an engineer, she became an opera singer and has sung in every opera house in the world. Then she became a builder. She helped with the rebuilding done after the tsunami and continues this work. I would certainly like to meet her one day.

We were starting to get a little worried about the Talpe property. We phoned LJS, and he said he would see us that evening. This made us decide to get a bus and go back to the property and try to see the owner. On the way, we discussed if we should give it a name as it appeared to have neither a name nor a number. "Hidden Haven," we thought, would be nice.

We left the bus far too early and had to walk past the house LJS has, and then down to "our" house. The gate was closed, but we could see into the garden. A car was in the driveway, and two men were working. No one took any notice of us. Even the two poor caged dogs did not bark. We could only see the front of the property, but at least three lovely trees had been cut down since we saw it just over a week before. I could have cried. Why would anyone cut down large fully grown trees, and one was a mango? We clung to the bars of the gate looking for a while and then turned to leave. We had hardly started walking away when a large car drove up as if to knock us down. LJS and a friend. This was a little odd as he had said he was not free until later that day, then decided we had misunderstood and the owner of the house had dictated the time. How though had he known where we were as had not told anyone of our plan. His nephew had seen us on the road and phoned LJS who then got his friend to leave his work, and they came to find us. Not sure why. After honking the horn, the foreman came up to the gate. They conversed together, and when the question of the cut-down trees came up, we were told that the trees were cut down in case they damaged the house! Utter nonsense, they had just been badly hacked down. The owner was now on the phone. No, we did not want air-conditioning, a three-piece suit, etc., but we would like to see inside the house and discuss things in person with the owner. There is a water meter, and the pressure is good. This is something Barbara had advised us to find out, to make sure we had piped water and not a well. We took her advice, though we did think we would prefer well water. We left with LJS and a friend, now feeling a little unsure of what was happening as there was still no agreement on when we could meet the owner and see the house. We were then taken to the air force restaurant on the beach at Koggale where we had been the day before. Nice place and cheap to eat with a buffet of rice and several curries. We intended to treat LJS and his friend as he had been so helpful, but as we sat down, he told us he had forgotten his wallet but that it would only cost us a pound and a piece. Evidently, it was assumed we would pay before we could offer. We were then driven to the Koggala bus station where we took a bus back to Galle. We spotted the Sydney Bar opposite the bus station in Galle and went in. I was the only woman, but the beer was cheap and cold. We discussed the events of the morning, cutting down the trees we could not understand, and we both felt upset about it. Michael was more optimistic and said we could buy our own and replant; I wondered if I would live long enough for it to grow into a beautiful tree. We both felt it odd that we still had not met the owner. LJS was charming, but we were puzzled why he found time to take us around, why he had come after us on learning we were going to look at the house again, and then the silly remark that he had forgotten his wallet, at which his friend had smiled and given a little laugh.

We phoned Barbara. After hearing our story about our dream house being refurbished and that we still had to sell our house, she said the owner would not wait for us. If we did get to rent it, he would want to sell it after the first year. She reiterated, as others had before, "Do not trust anyone," she had and regretted it. All rather sad news; we liked the people, knew Sita and her family, and Henry well by now, and trusted them completely.

At breakfast the following morning, we told friends who had given us Barbara's phone number how things stood. That we still did not know the name of the owner or the phone number, we all thought it a little odd. They said they were worried we would get ripped off, as we had not signed anything paid any money to anyone, we could not see how. Sita and her family also wanted to investigate the owner on our behalf and then suggested another option. They have a family home belonging to another of Sita's married daughters who has lived in Australia for the past 20 years. During this time, the house has remained empty. It had a large garden, and we could have it for free if we refurbished it. This sounded right up our street. We had enjoyed refurbishing the house we bought in the UK; it would be fun to do it again. The snag was it was inland from Colombo. We now had friends in the Galle area and enjoyed this part of the island. We arranged to catch the seven twenty-five train to Maradana, Colombo, the next morning. Sita's son would pick us up in a car and show us the property. We felt quite excited about it. To have a house we could remake was far better than taking over a perfect house designed by someone else.

We now had a day with no appointments so took a bus to Marrisa. The place we had enjoyed so much a few years before. We walked the length of the beach, a beach that before had been peaceful with few people. Now it had beach and surf cafés and extremely loud music, the sound of which travelled a very long way, disturbing all, and blotting out the sound of any natural life. Michael remembered the hut at the beginning of the lane that sold roti. This time the man running the hut had just two king coconuts which we enjoyed. We continued on to Amarasinghe guest house, but the delightful lane was no longer delightful with plenty of wildlife. The wildlife along the now polluted river had been replaced by many more guest houses. The garden of the rest house was still nice and more trees had been added with their name and usage clearly marked. Now perhaps a little bit too neat and tidy. We ordered a coffee. No other guests and the atmosphere did not feel the same. Not just because the sun was shining, we remembered the day of rain and sitting chatting to the English Buddhist and the Australian/Sri Lankan brother and sister. The owners we knew had been replaced with someone who appeared to have forgotten how to smile a long time ago. Just out of interest we asked how much the room we stayed in before was per night. Three thousand rupees, a big inflation in less than four years. We had paid eight hundred rupees. We left, still hearing the bass, thump, thump, of the music from the beach about two or three kilometres away. A young lad with a small catamaran wanted to take us for a trip on the lagoon for one thousand. It was an enjoyable trip with plenty of birds and water monitors spoiled only by the persistent noise from the beach.

Next day, we arranged to go and visit the house belonging to Sita's daughter and meet her son.

We walked to the station as not a single tuk-tuk in sight, where do they all go to in the night? Two and a half-hour train ride to Maradana, but we were in luck as we got seats and bought some wadi (small lentil pasties). Dilsulashon, Sita's son, was there and recognised us at once as the only white people alighting from the train. He was very nice and chatty just like his mother. The ride through Colombo was, as expected, like most cities, had nothing to recommend it, but once we got to Gampaha, green vegetation replaced concrete and we felt relaxed. The house could have been ideal, set back and in three acres, plenty of trees. Also, there was something strange which we were told was a brick maker. A huge cement mixer stood in front of the house as if on guard. It looked as if it intended to remain there but no doubt could be removed. The house, we felt, was charming and had a lot of possibility. It was large, mostly ground level, stairs led up to a large room giving onto a smaller one with a balcony. A lot of stored old furniture; I felt it would be fun to restore. The living area was nice but the ceiling false and needed taking out. A number of rooms but only one gritty bathroom.

A tiled roof but nothing below, and all needed doing as did the electric and plumbing. I would love to restore it, but Michael reminded me that we were twenty years younger when we did one in the UK and that roofing and actual building had not come into it. We also had no idea about how to go about getting workmen and equipment. Dilrulashan thought it would cost two hundred thousand rupees to have the main work done (about £1,000). That would be fine if it turned out, but we would need to go into it further. Had the house been in Galle, we might have jumped at it.

We had been fortunate with the journey there, but the return trip was dreadful. We were driven back to Colombo Fort, arriving forty minutes early. The platform was packed, and there was no place to sit. Over the loudspeakers, an announcement was made. Everyone rushed from platform five to six. We stood at the edge of the platform. The train arrived, and people were running alongside, trying to get in before it stopped. It came to a halt with a door right in front of us. The fact that now people had to alight before we could get on was not taken into account. A stampede of frightened animals was as nothing compared to the crowd wishing to get on the train. We were pushed aside as people fought each other to get a foothold on the train. Big men took advantage of their size, and the old, lame, women, and children were elbowed out of the way. People trying to get off had it no easier being blocked from getting off and pushed back by the crowd getting in. At the best of times, getting on was not so easy, the train being considerably higher than the platform. When we did get a chance, Michael pushed me up from behind and then prevented me from being pushed out again by alighting passengers. No chance of a seat. In that mass of humanity, we could not even see the seats. We tried to stay by the open door to get air but were propelled along by the crowd. Had there been someone with a gun, threatening to shoot anyone who did not get on, it could not have been worse. We had not been going long when I felt faint and needed to sit down and would have done so on the floor but squashed tight. A kind man gave me a seat. A little later, the man next to me got out, and Michael was able to take his seat. The nightmare had ended.

Back at Beach Haven, we were told that LJS and Asoka had both been phoning. We discussed how we got on and said how much we liked the house but did wonder if it was a bit ambitious of us to think we could get it shipshape and also we really wanted to be near Galle. However, the sister who owns it was coming from Australia soon, and we'll see what she says, so again nothing definite.

Next day off again to see yet another place, inland from Unawatuna. Past paddy fields, a nice area. A kindly well-spoken owner said there was one acre of land but it appeared to be much more with a not very attractive garden but lots of cinnamon trees, mangoes, coconuts, rambutans, limes, etc. The house is fine, four bedrooms and two bathrooms plus an annex. Very tempting, and he gave us his daughter's email address. When we asked about the rent, he had to think and came up with sixty thousand per month unfurnished and seventy furnished. £300 or £350.

We have now made a shortlist of the best: Talpe house, The Gingerbread One, Ahamgama, the house in Gampaha and the one we had just seen. The best, if we thought we could restore it, would be the one in Gampaha; that is, if it was in the Galle area. Talpe still was uppermost in our minds, but nothing seemed to be moving in that direction. It was now eleven days since we had first seen it and still did not even know the owner's name.

Later that day, Michael shot up as the phone rang. It had to be on him somewhere, but he had a number of pockets. Just as he found it, the ringing stopped. It rang again, and then the back of the phone came off and fell to the floor. It still worked, but he could not hear or understand. I took over and found we had LJS on the other end. The owner of the Talpe house was called Laxman, and he had his phone number – at last. I made the phone call and arranged we would meet him at the Royal Dutch café that afternoon. Laxman and his family went to Beach Haven instead, but we finally joined up. They wished to discuss things there, but we wanted to see the inside of the house. The problem was the large car was rather overfull with two sons, himself, and his wife. It was a squash, but we managed to all get in, which was roomy compared to the train, and set off finally to see the house properly.

Since the day when we had last seen it, a lot of work had been done. Trenches around the house were dug, and new water and sewage pipes were being put in. Three big bedrooms with good bathrooms, a water feature in the centre of the living area. Work was still taking place, but it looked good. He would not reduce the rent, but we could afford it. The two extra bedrooms over the garages were servants' quarters. It is a family home as most of the houses we found for rent were, and so not for sale. We gathered they have a number of other places. We told them we had yet to sell our house in the UK, they agreed to wait for us. We exchanged emails. We were so happy and relieved. We came back wishing to share our news with Sita and the family at Beach Haven, but they were all out. We went to Royal Dutch and told Fazal and Fatima our news and were given two garnets.

At breakfast, we shared our news with the family. Sita and Sharomi appeared pleased for us. We were not sure about Lalith; he disapproves of the amount of rent, saying it is too high. We had now been there 14 days and had, we felt found our future home.

Now we would just have to find a buyer for our house in the UK. Now that we had made up our minds, I felt sure that we would be able to sell. No longer needing to go house hunting, we decided to go to Kandy. This time we managed to alight at the correct station. My breathing was not so bad as before; I still got very tired but do so love walking. Michael was suffering with his hands. This was sad news as he suffered badly in England but was always gardening, and we put it down to something in the soil, plants, etc. Some doctors called it an allergy; others said it was an inherited disorder. The latter seemed more logical as we had been just over two weeks without doing any gardening. Now the skin was falling off his hands. We went to a shop for some cream, but when they saw his hands, the owner said he must go to a pharmacy. The owner then left his shop and took us to a pharmacy not too far off. Here they looked at his hands and promptly called a doctor; we were given chairs to sit and wait, but the doctor arrived not long after, apologizing for keeping us waiting. He prescribed three lots of pills and the same type of cream our doctor in the UK gives him. The pharmacy bill came to just over Rs.6,000, which rather shook us as in England we had never had to pay for pills, etc., it being free. The doctor said to just give Rs.6,000. He took nothing.

We did much as we had done on previous visits but felt now that the traffic around the lake had increased, making it less pleasant. At the tourist information, we were given a map and told we could walk to a large Buddha on a hill where there were views stretching for miles. We took a Tuk-tuk. A good view but the surrounding buildings were ugly. The Buddha stood 88ft high; it did not have the serene air about it as many of the older rock carvings, perhaps as brightly painted, but it was still hard to visualise just how they had made it, even in this day and age. We started walking back, stopping to sit on the edge of the road eating pineapple we had bought a Tuk-tuk driver who had given us his card the day before pulled up. We had planned to go to another hill on the opposite side of town to the Dawattakele forest. We took his tuk-tuk. As we arrived, Michael said, "We have been here before about three years ago." I believed him but was amazed as I could not remember it, and he is quite famous for not remembering places. It was a place I would have thought I could not forget as plenty of monkeys swinging about, toque monkeys, most of which were young ones enjoying exploring the forest, and a lot of jackfruit trees. The fruit of this tree can grow to become the largest fruit, so it is said, in the world. The monkeys were managing to twist the smaller ones off and letting them fall to the ground to burst open. The birds were resting in the heat of the day. Apart from the odd tweet, we neither saw nor heard them. Among the trees, a deer silently walked past not too far from us, and butterflies darted about. The tranquillity of the forest was the thing we enjoyed most, away from all the hustle and bustle and all the traffic. The single most remarkable item in the plant family was a huge Liana *Entada puseatha,* winding its way along the ground like some deformed petrified snake. We read that it was about 200 years old and spread over nearly two hectares. In search of insects, we turned over any rotting log we came across, never finding anything, except one leech, we moved off. On leaving the forest, we returned to our lodging. I felt something wet on my leg. Looking down, I saw one trouser leg now had a large patch of blood. To find the little bloodsucker, I pulled up the trouser leg. "No sign of a leech," I said. "No," said Michael, "It just dropped on my foot." He tossed it aside. Back at our lodgings, my leg was still bleeding. I washed the one leg of the trousers, and Michael stood on the bed to hang them up near the fan to dry. As he got down, we both noticed that now the bedsheet was covered in blood. While I washed the sheet, he examined his feet and found he was leaking from between his toes, but the leech must have dropped off. Later, Michael with a wad of paper between his toes and I, with one still damp trouser leg, went to a tiny place where they made vegetarian food. They had a couple of small tables. We sat at one and ate royally for Rs. 280 for both of us.

The Botanical Gardens was the following day's treat. We did a lot of dithering and walking, deciding how to get there, then we took a bus. As foreigners, it is not so cheap to visit the gardens – Rs. 1100 entrance fee each. I wondered how Sri Lankans who had been born abroad got on. I expect they got in as locals and they just take a look at our skin colour to brand us as foreigners. Not many countries would get away with such discrimination and felt sad that here it was normal for all fees to be ten times what the local people paid.

We spent the whole day in the gardens. There were other people but certainly not crowded, and in some areas we, and the monkeys, had to ourselves. The big bamboo, not indigenous to Sri Lanka, looked very much at home, and the monkeys loved them and the big concrete drain pipes that for some reason were there, where the monkeys had fun running in and out of them. A hare rushed across to some trees with a dog in hot pursuit, vanishing from sight. We held our breath but no screams; the hare got away. There was a lot more to the gardens than we had time to see on our previous visit. I spotted a large tree with buttresses looking so familiar. When up close, I read the sign. It was a Mora tree and had come from British Guiana, the country I had spent six happy years in. I also have a table made from a Mora tree buttress. It was a natural shape, but it was not until a Sri Lankan saw it and commented on its shape that I realised it was in the map of Sri Lanka, in reverse. The large ficus tree, one of the first things that had been pointed out to us previously, stood proudly spreading its branches unrestricted, as if saying "I am the king of trees and all must have a clear view of me." The orchids are breathtaking, though perhaps not in such large numbers and species as in Singapore. A Cannonball tree, another old South American friend. For the first time, I saw the Coco-de-mer, something I understood could not be grown outside the Seychelles, its natural home. The huge nut, possibly the largest seed in the world, looks like a Siamese twin coconut. Here stood several such palms, both male and female, their sex being very noticeable and so often laughed at as being the sexiest of plants, regardless that it is a late starter and does not flower until about 30 years old. Then the nut takes another ten years to ripen. I had seen a polished nut in the house of Bevis Bawa, whose house and garden are open to the public. An eye-catching ornament on a coffee table. Seeing the Talipot palms native to Sri Lanka, I realised for the first time where I had seen them before. In one of the West Indian islands in a botanical garden, I think Grenada, they had a number of Talipot. A few were in flower, and others were dying. They only live to flower once before they die, I collected seeds to make into jewellery. I liked to know the names of the seeds I used, even if it was only the local name, but in this, the staff could not help me. These palms had been planted many years before by the British, and sadly all records of the plants in the gardens had been lost in a fire. All they knew was that they came from another country. That country must have been Sri Lanka. Though I had seen them before in various parts of this country and knew that the young leaves were bleached and used to write on with a stylus, then the pages bound together and the cover made from wood as were all the sacred books in temples, I had not remembered the West Indian ones until this time, seeing them with flowers, the seeds, and then dyeing. It was extraordinary that after about 35 years, I had an answer to my question. It was not only the plants that gave us such pleasure, and there were also books for sale. Books I would love to own but restrained from buying, knowing it would be crazy to buy them, take to England, pack, and return. All in all, it had turned out to be a wonderful day.

That evening, Henry rang. We had arranged to visit him in Bentota on Sunday. He now suggested Tuesday as work was being done and there was a strong smell of paint. Dinner again was Masala Dose and would have been followed up by espresso coffee at a new place we had found, only it was closed.

Back in Galle, we finally unearthed the phone. People were already getting a bit tired of us not answering their calls. Everyone, it appeared, kept their phones on their person, so handy every time it rang. We never attained that state of sophistication. Nor did we know that when given a person's phone number, we could enter it into the phone so when they phoned, we knew who we were talking to, which is, we had to admit, a big advantage. Seeing we had four missed calls, I had a go at phoning them back. One sounded very nice, but I had no idea who he was; he wanted to know if there was anything he could do for us and sent his regards to Michael. I did inquire twice as to who I was speaking to, but if I was told, I did not hear. Our future landlord also phoned and wished to invite us to dinner, which was very kind, and we would have loved to accept but for the fact we would have left Sri Lanka before that date. I asked if we had to sign or do anything before we left, "No, we can keep in touch by E-mail." LJS phoned saying he would be in Colombo on Tuesday and would go to the immigration with us. We felt surrounded by kind and helpful people. At The Royal Dutch, we were given a tobacco leaf we had requested a man to get for us, having failed to find one to buy. We thought he had forgotten but had delivered it to Fazal. Fazal then invited us to dinner with him on Monday.

After enjoying a few days of looking around, seeing friends, etc., we were ready to leave Galle. Said goodbye to Sita, Sharome, and her daughter, expressing our hope that we would soon be returning. We went by bus to Bentota where we visited Henry and Thersia. Their house, which we felt was perfect before, had now undergone so much work, turning it into quite a palace. We felt bad that they had been up all night preparing our room, but they gave us a lovely welcome. My bedroom was wonderful, with the biggest bed I had ever seen, 6' x 7'. Henry was turning his home into a place for tourists to stay, and these days tourists are getting rather large, so more space is needed. We sat around the pool he had made, 4' 6" deep, as some rule said it could not be any deeper. Kingfishers kept diving in for a splash, and parakeets were happily enjoying the food put out for them. Then we saw our first paradise flycatcher, with a black head, pure white body, and the longest thin tail that rippled as it flew. That evening, a Dutchman, Tito, joined us for dinner. We learned from him about some of the obstacles we would have to surmount to get a resident visa, which we would need before we could rent a place or have a bank account. We would have to get police clearance and also have health insurance. We would have a visa called the "My Dream Home" visa; he was not joking. Living, as we discovered, was cheap, but the amount of money we would have to put in our bank account every month was eight times more than our joint pensions. Yes, we certainly did need to sell our house, as we also had to show we had a lot of money in the bank in the UK. Living in Paradise evidently did not come cheap.

We left early the following morning to meet, as arranged, LJS and go to the immigration office.

When the train stopped at Fort, I phoned LJS, telling him we would soon arrive at Maradana. Apparently, he did not hear. We stood outside the station for some time, phoned LJS again. There was such a noise I could not tell if he understood or not. When he did arrive, he was not very pleased. He had been in the area dropping his wife off and had passed the station but not seen us as he expected, thinking we would be at Colombo Fort station. "All foreigners go there," he told us. "Well, not if they wished to go to the immigration office which was only down the road a bit from Maradana." He dropped us off outside a well-marked door and went to park. To our dismay, the door had a padlock and chain. A man standing nearby told us to go a bit further and through a complex of shops and restaurants and take a lift to the third floor. It was a little strange that LJS had not known this. As it turned out, this venue was well-established but as yet no one had thought to change the signs. There was no sign of LJS, and owing to his size, he would have been hard to miss. The place was crowded, with a lot of tourists wishing to get extensions on their visas. Our phone rang, LJS enquiring as to where we were. On being told we were on the third floor, which was the visa place, he informed us he was also on the third floor by the lifts. He was looking at a sign that said 3rd Floor but missed seeing the arrow pointing to the stairs. We started to wonder who was leading whom. When our number was called, we went in alone. We had expected him to come with us as a warrantor; if not, we saw no point in him accompanying us. We asked for details on how to get a resident visa. Another man was called; he hunted around for the paper, went out, and returned with it.

He told us we would need to have $3,000 per month. I said I had understood it would be $1,500 for one of us and $750 for the other. He consulted with another man and then agreed and actually wrote it down on a piece of paper. We could not have a bank account until we got the visa and would not get a visa until we proved we had the money. That was that.

LJS gave us a tour of the nicer part of the city. We visited another toy factory and loaded a pile of folded cardboard boxes. After that, he kindly drove us to Negombo to the place we had stayed in before. Over a beer, he told us that when we came back with a shipment of our possessions, he would do all the paperwork and get us cleared through customs. As an importer and exporter, he knew all the rules. He would keep an eye on the property we wanted, and when we came back, meet us at the airport. How fortunate could we be to have fallen in with such a kind and helpful friend?

Having expected to spend two or three days getting a visa, we were now left with three days to fill before catching a plane back to the UK. This time we were keen to get home and put our house back on the market. Everything so far was working out so well that I felt confident this time we would find a buyer. Michael said I was being optimistic.

I felt we were destined to have the Talpe house; it would have to happen. We filled our time seeing new places, a boat ride on the wetlands via the canal. The two-hour excursion was filled with a wonderful variety of birds, from coots and herons to the beautiful bee-eaters.

That evening, we were given a local English language newspaper; Nelson Mandela had died three days before, aged 95. Not unexpected but still very sad.

We had walked and seen all there appeared to be, which in the main was Catholic churches and places spoiled with masses of garbage and often firecrackers. The beggars, fortunately, had given up on us. We still felt that we enjoyed Buddhist areas the most. Wishing to see just a bit more before we left, we asked Buddika from Serendip Tours to take us further inland to any place he thought might be of interest to us. In no time, we were in the countryside, which gave us a much more charitable idea of Negombo. We visited a cave temple after Buddika had found the caretaker to open the door. Though a Christian, Buddika knew a lot about the Buddhist way of life. As before, there were paintings and statues of Buddha, all with white faces and just one with a black face. The white faces denoted that the Buddha had been very good in his past life, the black one wicked. Very odd in a land with dark-skinned people. We told Buddika, jokingly, that we must have been very good but he wicked in our former lives. The trees in the surrounding garden interested me. A Peepal or Bo tree, the most sacred of trees. The most eye-catching tree to us was a Nar tree or ironwood tree, the national tree of Sri Lanka, so we were told, but the Talipot Palm had also been quoted thus. The Nar tree is a beautiful tree with drooping branches; the new leaves are tipped in red.

When in flower, the white flowers hang down on thread-like stems. Two monks sat under its branches meditating, and we sheltered from a light shower. We stopped at a fibre factory, an open-air place with coconut husks soaking in water before using a simple machine that processes it ready for making into string, mats, brooms, etc. This results in a lot of fine dust left behind, which is made up into grow bags or compost. The coconut palm must be the most versatile and useful plant in the world.

Next, we entered a temple through the open jaws of a lion's mouth. This was a wonderland, almost Disney-like. Large, brightly painted figures, all three-dimensional. Two men were touching up the paintwork. It was all rather magical. The stages of a man's life were depicted: a newly born baby, a child at school, a grown man, marriage, his children, then an old man, and finally death. I did wonder if the same scene was ever depicted using female figures.

We had one last thing to find before we left. I wanted to buy some or even just one beedi, the poor man's smoke. So common once in India and Sri Lanka. We had not seen a single one in our recent trips, for sale or being smoked. The day before we left, Michael suggested we ask at a very small shop. He himself had never seen one but must have had a feeling this would result in success. With little hope on my behalf, I asked. At first, they did not feel sure and discussed among themselves and then asked how many. Many years ago, I had been a smoker and bought them in bundles. Here I was shown a few loose ones, rather smaller than I remembered. I could have ten for ten rupees. About to pay, they changed their minds; it was Rs. 20 and quickly that changed to Rs. 30. We gave them all our loose change, Rs. 28. They then gave us two rupees back and gave us eight beedis. We failed to understand their calculations but were happy to have at last got our hands on some. They would be a fun gift along with the tobacco leaf for a friend who was interested in all natural things and was trying to grow tobacco in her English garden.

Chapter Twelve

Selling and Packing

Bats like being packed together

My optimism that we would get a buyer for our house, now that we had found our dream home in Sri Lanka, was not wrong. We put it back on the market, and as soon as the advert came out, we had two interested parties. We accepted an offer and set to packing boxes of books. Our future landlord was being emailed as events took place, making sure we still would have the Talpe property. His answers reassured us. LJS wrote asking us to send photocopies of all the pages in our passport and police clearance; then he would get our visa for us. This was a big surprise, as we understood we had to go in person and show bank balance, etc. We sent what he asked for. Having nearly sold the house the year before, we had sold most of the things we would not be taking with us. What we still had and did not need, the buyers agreed to buy. We obtained estimates from several packers, all had the first name David. One was very helpful as he was used to sending things to Sri Lanka and knew all the ins and outs and had delivery contacts in Colombo. He gave us a list of things we could take or not. We put our camper van up for sale; it was 25 years old, and we could only bring in a car less than three years old. In hindsight, we should have used that agent and saved ourselves a lot of stress and money, but we felt after all the kindness of LJS with his offer of doing all clearance, etc., it would be rude not to take him up on it. Our arrangement was to have packers in to pack everything, excepting books for which they gave us the boxes, and I packed. Then they would hold it in storage until the time to put it on a ship. Give us details of arrival, and after that, it was up to us. We had to insure the whole shipment, which was all in a large container. We do not believe in insurance, so put a low value. After all, we would never be able to replace a thousand books, carvings, etc., from many lands, diaries, and photos. All that we valued could not be compensated for with money. Thinking we would no longer be repairing things, we put most of the tools up for sale. Everything was snapped up except a long three-length ladder. We decided to have it packed. My guardian angel was still with us. That ladder has been more than useful to us and neighbours.

Selling a house is not done overnight. The buyer had the money and wished to move in. We were ready to move out, but the whole business with lawyers involved took a couple of months. We held our breath that the house in Sri Lanka would still be available. When a date was finally arranged for the handing over of the keys, we booked a flight intending to leave the same day. We changed the date on finding that it was cheaper to fly on Sunday, and our friend Betty, living almost opposite, had kindly offered to let us stay in her house until we left. At the time, we never guessed what a lucky thing waiting until Sunday would turn out to be...

The day dawned. We had to stay in the house until the agent informed us that the buyer's money had come and been put in our bank account. The last boxes were taken out, the new owners arrived, and we moved across the road. This time we would not be travelling light. We had bought two suitcases at a charity shop which were packed with essentials like our Italian coffee pot, sheets, pillows, and a few cacti that I figured would be able to stand the journey. One quite large cactus picked up in Italy and a few small ones bought in France. We had one more important transaction: to get a copy of our bank account showing how rich we were, to enable us to get the required resident visa. The bank printed out the statement as requested. It had the same amount showing as before we sold, correction £45 less, which was payment for the money to be put directly into the bank on exchange of keys. The bank was helpful but assured us the house money had not been put in. Next, a visit to the agent where we were told it was all handled by the solicitors. The solicitors were positive that they had transferred the money. The bank and solicitor contacted each other.

This huge amount of money had vanished into space! A little worrying to say the least. The next day was spent going back and forth between solicitors and the bank trying to find out where our money had gone. Checking our bank statement yet again, we saw we had been credited the £45 they had deducted for fast transfer. This was no joke; we needed the thousands we had sold the house for. The bank was sympathetic. We had explained why we needed the statement showing we had the money before flying off on Sunday. They took Betty's phone number, promising to phone us when the money was found.

Just before five on Friday night, the phone rang to say it was now all sorted, and we could get our bank statement the following morning. We almost collapsed with relief.

When we learned the facts, we felt it was astonishing that a country like England could make such a mess of things. The solicitor had been at fault; in the space for our bank account number, they had put their file number.

We were at the bank as it opened on Saturday. By now, all the staff knew the story of the missing thousands, and all were smiles when we entered, wishing us well as they had also been told why it was so important to get the money showing on our statement.

There was one other small hitch we feared might give us trouble. I had got our visitors' visas online; it was easy and all was well until a few days before we left when they thought to tell us that we must show a return or forward airline ticket. Not intending to leave, we had bought singles.

Sunday morning, Betty and another friend helped us drag the two suitcases to the bus station. Goodbyes were said, and we were on our way.

We turned to each other, "Happy?" we asked in unison. We stopped smiling before reaching Heathrow. We had shared a pecan pasty and, more stupidly, tried to read a newspaper we had bought. A fatal thing to do if you suffer from travel sickness. We both feel very ill.

On arrival at Heathrow, when we were getting the cases out, I tripped over the kerb and went sprawling. Michael, next to me, never noticed. A man got me back on my feet; my knee hurt but the skin was not broken. A little later, Michael, not to be outdone, hit his shin and made it bleed.

We had expected to meet Fiona, our niece, at Café Royal in the airport. She was there, along with her husband, Jim, and son, Oscar, Jennie, our sister, and her husband, Ian. A lovely surprise for us. We enjoyed a last meal with the family before checking in. That really made our day.

Going through security, Michael was held back. His glasses case was metal and had set the alarm bells ringing. Next, they made him remove his shoes. After collecting our hand luggage, we moved off. Michael came to a stop, "Where are my shoes?" He had just discovered he was walking in his socks. Going back, we found his shoes. "Let's get out of here before anything else goes wrong."

Peacock looks beautiful even when not displaying

Chapter Thirteen

Sri Lanka: Ups and Downs

All went well on arrival. No one asked to see our return ticket or check our bags for cacti. LJS was there as promised, waiting for us. We were taken to his home to meet his son and wife. A very nice place with a splendid staircase to the third floor. We had our own room and bathroom on the ground floor. We showered and fell asleep. We felt so lucky having met such a helpful person.

We soon felt even more indebted to LJS. He drove us around all day. First, the immigration and a long wait until shown into a room, only to be told it was not the room we needed. Back for another long wait. We had assumed we would be given the same rules as for a husband and wife, as before they had agreed to our argument. Now we were told they could not change the rules for us, and we would both have to bring in a thousand pounds a month. We would be given separate visas and had to have more photos. I thought we knew this and had plenty of passport-size photos, but Michael said he did not think he had brought his. The first thing was to get health insurance, which was required before they could issue a visa. LJS, as usual, had not come in with us. When told about having to get insurance, he did a lot of phoning. Then a long drive to sit on chairs for a couple of hours while a man rang around every insurance company in the country, only to be told by all that we were too old. Too old by far as they were not interested in anyone over sixty. Back with this news to immigration. The same man who had sent us off on this wild goose chase now hands me a paper with a government insurer address. Why, we wondered, could he have not done so before. We were puzzled why LJS did not know this or ever come into the offices with us, understanding he knew all the procedures. The insurance place was nearby, and we soon came away with our insurance papers and a much lighter purse. Tomorrow we would start again.

After a beer on the verandah, followed by a splendid meal cooked by LJS's wife, Michael sorted out all his papers and found he had plenty of passport-sized photos. All was well with the world. Happy and well-fed, we dropped off to sleep as our heads touched the pillows.

When we dropped off LJS's wife at her place of work, she took the copies of our passports and got them verified and stamped. Armed now with all these papers, we went back to immigration. As we sat down in the correct room, we were each given a sheet of paper to write a letter requesting a visa. We were soon to learn that all institutions, banks, etc., liked you to write a letter, regardless of the fact you had filled in the required forms. A man disappeared with all the relevant papers. Later, he gave our passports back and told us to return on Friday to receive a paper that would allow us to open a bank account.

We had achieved all we could for the time being and so would now go to Galle. LJS first showed us where the highway bus was and where we could get a bus to his place. He asked if we could find it again. We doubtfully said, "Maybe."

LJS needed to go to his factory and so drove us to Galle on the new highway which had only recently been opened. Amazingly, it was almost free of traffic, nice smooth tarmac, and very little litter. Best of all, no dead bodies until almost reaching Galle, when we saw a squashed monitor lizard. LJS said that nobody liked killing animals but when the road first opened, motorists, who until then had never been able to test out how fast they could go, owing to all the traffic, then sped and found they could not stop in time when an animal crossed the road.

Returning to Beach Haven felt like coming home. Sita was there, but not well; she had asthma, and Shiromi was in Colombo. The chocolate we had bought for Sita at the airport was very soft, and a chocolate rabbit for the wee girl opposite had turned into a liquid mess in my bag, while, for some reason, the Smarties were OK.

We were dropped off at the Fort agreeing to meet LJS at six. He would then show us the only rooftop garden in Galle. Later, six was changed to seven. We ate, waited, went for a walk, and found the artist's place he had described. When LJS arrived, we were told he had gone to Beach Haven to pick us up. Not for the first time, we noted people with transport rarely walked. From the shop full of paintings, we climbed the stairs to a garden complete with a pond and a couple of tortoises.

The owner waters his garden every morning. It was a pleasant place overlooking that part of the Fort. The mosque was nearby, and we heard the call for prayer. The Buddhist friends we were with complained bitterly and said it should not be allowed as it disturbed the peace. We would remember this remark in the future when the loudspeakers from the Buddhist temples would often produce talking and chanting drums, etc., all day.

LJS had introduced us to his bank manager. We went to sleep that night feeling that we had at last cracked the official stick.

One thing bothered us: we desperately wanted to contact the owner of our home-to-be. I had brought my laptop with me and emailed him, waiting for a reply. When it did come, he wrote that the house was almost finished. This was a surprise as he had originally said it would be finished before the New Year, and now it was March. He added that we could move in or stay with him rent-free until it was finished. Nice of him, but we felt we should get solicitors together first. While eating our dinner at the Indian Hut, which had now been extended and changed quite a bit since our last visit, we looked down and saw LJS. He came up. He thought it would be OK to move in as no money was involved. We agreed we would like to. LJS was going back to Colombo the next morning but arranged for a friend of his to drive us and our luggage to the Talpe house. He then phoned the landlord who said it was not possible until next week as it was not finished!

On the appointed Friday, Michael said he did not mind going to immigration by train on his own to collect the note allowing us to open a bank account. He did well, though a long day and had walked from the station to the immigration office, finding it further than remembered.

At the bank the next day, we had lengthy discussions with the bank agreeing to bring in a large amount of sterling. They appeared hungry for sterling and thought it best if we transferred all we had in the UK to the bank here. We did not agree, but would bring in one hundred thousand pounds to be split between us as they said we could not have joint accounts as we were foreigners. A little odd, it seemed to us. We were given account numbers so I could transfer the amounts straight into our respective accounts. It sounded easy but proved a little more difficult.

Sharomi had given me their online address but found it hard to input. Her son tried, and he also failed, but then after we stopped, it worked, perhaps we were too impatient. Then I did all that was required to transfer the money, but it would not move on as they needed a phone number. Ours was broken, and I did not know the number anyway. I put in LJS's number, and the request went..

We were impatient to get into our new home and failed to understand the delay. To kill time, we went to several nearby places. We went again to Unawatuna. Brian, our cousin's son, was back in the UK, and his business partner Asoka was not there. Michael decided we should take a shortcut. His shortcuts are famous for taking twice as long, but I went along with the idea. We headed inland and soon realised our mistake. Handing Michael my bag, I took a wee in the vegetation. When he handed it back, I noticed he did not have his bag. Apparently, according to him, I should have noticed before. Back we went and found his bag still hanging on a chair at B's place. Setting out again, we went the regular way and then took a Tuk-tuk back to the Fort. In the Tuk-tuk, I asked Michael where his bag was; he showed me it was hanging in front of him. We got out at Beach Haven, and Michael paid and followed me in. Suddenly, he shouted, "My bag!" and went racing off down the road, yelling "STOP!" A man on a scooter asked what his problem was. On being told, he let Michael get on the back of his scooter, and they set off in hot pursuit of the red Tuk-tuk and his bag. By then, he was not sure if the red Tuk-tuk that came in sight was the same one. He was in luck; it was the correct Tuk-tuk, and his bag was hanging where he had left it. The driver said he should not have panicked as he knew where we were and would have returned it. What if another passenger had got in before he discovered it.

Sita was feeling much better, and we sat talking until LJS arrived in a nice small car.

He had said he was going to take us to get our phone repaired. It was a secondhand phone we were pressed into buying on a previous trip. Now he said he had not got it with him, so he would buy us a new one. We protested; we did not want a new one, and if we did, we would pay for it. We were in their hands; we purchased a phone for Rs. 2,600. Then, given a long lesson on how it worked. We never saw our old one again.

Now at long last, after six days of waiting, we were going to see our future home. When we stopped outside, for a moment we thought it was the wrong house. Devastation! The house now looked much nearer to the road. It boasted a nice large patio, which was the improvement that we had expected. It was the garden that we loved so, as such it hardly remained, just piles of sand and rubble in front of the house. Trees had vanished. While the new patio was nice, it had a fence made of cement to resemble wood. Another such fence dividing the now clear land from a little remaining vegetation. With all the trees they had cut down, one would have thought a wooden fence, if there had to be one, would have been easy. I told myself we could disguise it with plants. Evidently, once started on "improvement", the owner had found it hard to stop. I hate the word "security", and here they are mad on it. The wall round the front of the property had been eight feet high, which surely was high enough, but now it was being extended. We walked to the back. The land that had been boggy and full of vegetation had now been cleared, bare earth and the river at the end fenced off. We had so looked forward to this area, feeling it would be a wonderful place to find insects and aquatic life. I was almost in tears by then. The owner cheerfully said he had plans and was going to plant an orchard of fruit and spice trees. We were taken into the house that before had been, or so we thought, complete. Now no longer clean, one bedroom stuffed high with furniture. Wall lights and one-inch-deep inlets in the walls probably for family photos they are so keen on. Turning to Michael, I said, "Where could we put bookshelves and pictures?" He shook his head. "You could not hang up Moroccan lamps either," he pointed out. The kitchen appeared to no longer have a place to cook, which surely is the normal thing to do in a kitchen. The big chimney had been closed and was now a cupboard. The house was a disappointment, but it was the garden that upset us the most, so changed and no longer the delightful place that we had first seen. We felt committed. Our stuff was on its way, and our visa soon to be granted. Our gloomy looks prompted the owner to say two bedrooms and the kitchen would be cleaned, and we could move in rent-free the following weekend. In the hope of finding something we liked, we asked about the two-bed and bathroom annex. Rather late in the day, we were told that was not included. What we did have to have was a watchman which we would pay. We did not want a watchman; we did not fancy being watched, and he spoke no English. We could have the use of one garage, but he wanted the other for storage. Then the dogs were added. Two poor large dogs who I had talked to while they were in a cage. One acted as if he hated me, and the other ignored me. I said if we had them, they would not be kept in a cage. The owner said they were only caged because the workmen were afraid of them. The completion date was now the end of March; we doubted it. When we pointed out that he had told us all would be finished by New Year, he said the workmen very often did not turn up and now it was very hard to get anyone to work. Rather a shame he had got them to ruin all that they did.

Our dream bubble had now burst. I felt like weeping.

LJS now suggested we go to Dieter in Unawatuna to eat. On arriving, we were told he only had one gas ring working, a load of people, and no food left. We downed a beer and left. For us, it did not matter; we were in no mood to celebrate. We wanted to go back to Beach Haven, but LJS and a friend had other ideas, and we found ourselves on the beach at one of the numerous cafés. They ordered food and sat chatting together. Our food had to come from the vegetarian restaurant. We, as expected, paid for everything, by then past caring.

Sleep did not come the following night. We either stayed silent or kept discussing the shock we had on seeing our dream home. Three months of being so excited thinking it was all we wanted and now after our visit the bubble had burst. The more we talked it over, the more upset I became. Why had we agreed to move in at the weekend? "We do not have to take it, we had not signed or paid anything," Michael pointed out.

Feeling we must do something, we decided to phone the landlord in the morning. Michael hates the phone, but we both felt it would be best if he phoned. Michael phoned but could not hear properly, so I took over. Another meeting was suggested. The landlord seemed to think we would not remember how to get to his place. Did we look that stupid? Later, LJS phoned and said we would go there that evening.

It was Tuesday, and Sita opened a big cake tin to dole out money to people who were in real need and came to collect it. Donors sent money from the UK and Holland, and the recipients wrote airmail thank-you letters. Sita was just a few years older than me but had a wonderfully productive life and was still helping people.

Back at the house that evening, it did not seem as awful as it had the day before. Michael is not keen on having a dog as he is allergic to them, and we were told that they would take the dogs, so we need not have them. More furniture had appeared, including some really nice stuff. The kitchen now had electric sockets. The water feature in the living area now had an added fountain, though not yet working, and I was not sure about that; it was starting to look a little too ornate.

I felt a little frightened when he said if we did not like it, that was OK; we did not have to have it. Still, with the picture of what it had looked like in my mind, I now felt I did want it. The watchman, we were told, did not live in what we had been told were the servants' quarters but in a hut in the garden. As labour was hard to get, we would be unlikely to get a maid. We could turn one of the rooms into a guest room, and we could have one garage for tools and a bike. He picked up on the word bike and was surprised Michael had one. I spotted what was a lovely old couch but with the cane work broken. I said to leave it; I would repair it. Again, he was surprised, probably thinking we were a lower class of humans than he had at first taken us for. The upper class mostly prefers to be known for not repairing things or riding a bike. So, missing a lot of fun in life.

The first thing to make us smile on that visit was a small cow in the garden, a soft brown colour with big eyes. She belonged to the watchman. Then we saw the monkeys were still in the remaining trees. Perhaps out of necessity, we started to accept all the changes and agreed we would come at the weekend. The landlord, who had suggested we do so in the first place, now said it would be better to wait until it was all finished. It hardly mattered, but I was dying to start on the garden, plant my cacti to give them better living conditions. The big Italian cactus had already—with relief at being released from a box—grown another section.

A third friend of LJS we found very nice and easy to talk to. Unable to pronounce his name correctly, we called him Manny. He told us how LJS had built up a very good business but lost it all in the tsunami. We should perhaps overlook some of his odd ways. That evening, Michael and I felt much happier.

The following days were spent pricing burners to cook on and a fridge. I bought a clay cooking pot, a sieve, and a coconut spoon. LJS phoned; bad line, but he said, "See you later." It was surprising that he was back in Galle. After waiting some time, we phoned him. He was in Colombo!

Checked emails and had an urgent one from our bank in Galle. The money transferred to Michael's account was fine. Mine, for some odd reason, they had sent to Angela Hargreave, a combination of our two names, so of course, it did not match the name in my passport. I sent two messages to get it amended.

Next day, another message from the Galle bank said it was urgent for the UK bank to get the name correct. I sent off another email. We wandered around town; it was becoming very familiar territory now. We saw Chamara Sampath, still very young looking and still jumping off Flag Rock into the sea. A very brave young man; we just hope he lives to be an old one.

We watched for turtles when it was high tide. No turtles were to be seen, but it was a pleasant place to sit in a strong breeze. We waited for the sun to set. The big red globe got lower and lower, moving far faster than in the northern climes. Just after six, it hid behind a cloud. We left, and I tried to phone the bank in the UK, without success.

Next morning, LJS arrived and said we should go house hunting! Odd as we thought we had come to an agreement with the Talpe house. With nothing better to do, we agreed. After showing us a few unattractive houses, he said he knew a German lady with a house; he phoned her. She told him she was in Colombo. That was not the end of it. "We will see," LJS grinned. Arriving, we found the gate closed, but as he pointed out, it was locked from the inside, so he commenced to honk his horn. The lady opened up, but we sensed she was none too pleased to see him. We felt both embarrassed and confused. The house was for sale, not for rent, and also not in any way suitable for us. The owner was nice, but LJS behaved in the most odd manner, marching from room to room as if he owned it. We managed to talk to the owner and said we only wished to rent, so we were not sure why he had brought us to her house. About to leave, LJS climbed up a Jambu tree and started picking the fruit. The owner begged him to come down as he was large, and the tree might break, and she had a basket of the fruit he could have. We watched, tongue-tied; he was acting like a naughty little boy. Ignoring her pleas and filling his pockets with the fruit. What had got into him? Not for the first time, we were puzzled by his strange behaviour.

One house we were shown had the most wonderful land, and we would have taken it, house unseen, but the owner was out and the house was for sale. Yet another, the owner was in the States. It all seemed a rather senseless waste of time; surely, if he knew about these houses, he would have also known they were not for rent or the owners unavailable. Before returning to Galle, all the stolen fruit was given to a young boy.

We emailed the landlord of the Talpe house, saying we would come tomorrow and stay for free until the work was completed, and confirmed an agreement that we would have the use of one of the servant rooms and a garage.

Still no word from the bank in the UK. The Galle bank still keeps asking to clear the matter up. Michael had all his bank accounts settled.

Still no reply from the landlord the following day. LJS said he was coming at nine and we had understood that his friend was taking us out at nine thirty. While waiting, I checked to see if there was anything from the bank. The only email I found contained five photos of a house and surrounding land. It looked nice, but it had a 'For Sale' notice.

Things were getting rather unreal, like an odd dream. We were never sure just what was happening. As we had not heard from the landlord, we could hardly turn up to stay and were starting to think we would never get the house. We gave up waiting and were about to go out on our own when LJS turned up. He then took us to an almost hidden house, off the end of the highway which we had seen from the road the day before. The one for sale that he had sent a picture of. The Talpe house was forgotten. We fell in love with this colonial-type house set in two and a half acres. We could, from the front, just see the road. The land had been a coconut plantation but with many other fruit trees and all very overgrown. My hands itched to get working on it. It was not flat, the land far from it, but I pushed that to the back of my mind. The house was very clean and in perfect condition, looked as if it had just been redecorated.

Living area, four bedrooms, three bathrooms, and in the courtyard a modern and a traditional kitchen and numerous other rooms and buildings. We were told a watchman went with the house but we could pay him with coconuts! Was it a joke? He could not speak English but had a dog trailing him, who I have to admit I thought looked a bit like a hyena and had a bad case of mange. That Bandusena, this watchman, could love this strange little dog I felt was a good reference. Why we would want a watchman I had no idea but if his pay was just coconuts it hardly mattered. LJS told us he had talked the owners into renting rather than trying to sell the house. He now tried to phone them with no luck. Back in Galle, we kept our fingers crossed. All thought of what had once been our dream home in Talpe vanished. The Walahanduwa house was what we really dreamed of having. It was unbelievable, we loved it. We agreed it just had to be the home we were looking for.

There was an open-air music festival at the moon bastion of the Fort that evening. With still no news from the bank in the UK, or the Talpe landlord, we decided to go along and sit on the grass listening to the groups perform. A Bangladeshi group had just started their performance when the phone rang. I could hardly hear with all the noise and music but heard enough to know that the house could be ours. Surely, the best news we had heard since returning to Sri Lanka.

We left the noise and the music to find a quieter spot to phone back. We had just stepped onto the road when we were spotted by LJS's friend on a motorbike. He and LJS had a knack of sniffing us out. We were told we needed copies of our passports. I got on the back of the bike to return to Beach Haven, leaving Michael to walk the short distance. Fortunately, we had made several copies. I found mine, and Michael found his. We were almost shaking with excitement. We then went to a café to wait for LJS.

The deal was outlined. The rent was considerably less than the Talpe house, though still high according to other people. We keep the watchman, the delightful bit is, they assured us again we pay him in coconuts! At first thought, this was a joke, but they insisted it was the case. We would have a contract to show Lalith. The house we understood was owned by someone in the States, but his mother lives in Colombo and will act on his behalf. LJS phoned the son, and he sounded nice and agreeable to let us rent. The thing now is to get my bank account sorted on Monday. Then get our visa. They asked for two years' rent in advance. Lalith had told us not to pay more than one year in advance.

The owner will pay for gas burners, fans, mattresses, etc. I suggested we would like to move in by Wednesday as it would be my 77th birthday. I am not that keen on birthdays, having had so many, but it made a good excuse to get in as soon as possible.

That evening, I looked at emails and found a rather belated one from the landlord in Talpe, saying we could come the next day. I felt it best not to answer until we were assured of this other house. The UK bank just said that my details were correct!

My Cacti

Mongoose

Cobra

I was then very excited. Michael, being more practical, kept looking at the negative points of view. Two years' rent was a lot. I had always said I wanted a lot of land, but flat, and the land there was anything but flat. Michael had, on our first visit, made me walk up the driveway. No problem, I could still breathe. There were many flat parts on the land, and I loved it all.

The next day, Sunday, we were invited to go and have dinner at LJS's friend's house. We like him a lot. He did not say much but appeared more thoughtful and genuine.

In the afternoon, I went to the Walahanduwa house. I took the cacti, feeling they deserved a bit of soil after over two weeks. A little bit crazy as we had still not made any formal agreement or even met the family that owned it. Deep down, I was placing our claim on the house. This time it had to be ours. The watchman, Bandusena, seeing me place them near a nam-nam tree in the courtyard, dug the dry earth with a heavy-looking crowbar and watered them. An unasked, thoughtful act.

The two larger bedrooms had a shared bathroom, so we thought we would use the smaller ones which had a bathroom each. I felt the house could wait and went out into the garden, seeing a monitor lizard and a number of palm squirrels and birds. No monkeys, but I was assured they would come. I could not resist doing a bit of hand gardening, releasing shrubs from being strangled by vines. I noticed this house also had dogs but free, no sign of a cage, and Bandusena appeared very fond of the one small dog that did not have much to recommend it, with a clipped ear – I later learned that was to show it had been neutered – the one I privately called Hyena. It followed him around devotedly. Also, a black dog looking pregnant. LJS said it was only because Bandusena fed them. The information that we paid Bandusena in coconuts proved to be a bit of an exaggeration. We pay in Rupees, but we also have the rights to all the coconuts. If we have them picked and sell them, it will, so LJS now says, the profit will pay Bandusena's wages.

That evening, we had a very nice meal at the friend's house, with lots of vegetarian dishes that were all very enjoyable. At the time, we found it a little strange that his wife and young daughters did not join us, but sat in front of a television while the wife spoon-fed the younger seven-year-old daughter. We soon discovered that this was not strange. When invited to dine in anyone's homes, we would usually eat alone. Occasionally, the husband might join us, but not the wife. Also, children quite capable of feeding themselves, especially as it's easier when they use their hands, are often spoon-fed. We Noticed mothers are often seen lifting and carrying both boys and girls of school age. They do not object, even in front of their friends. While eating, the phone rang. It was the lawyer for the owners of the house. We were informed that as foreigners - we got to hate this word 'foreigner' - we will have to pay an extra government tax. It did not amount to much. I doubted we would get in by Wednesday, so many unexpected little things to do.

First thing on Monday, we went to the bank. Still no amendment of my name. Michael's account is OK; he just had to sign lots of papers. Apparently, the bank had sent a letter to us at the Talpe address we had given them, not unreasonable except we no longer wish to rent it. Later in the day, an email from our bank at last. Apologies for not replying and saying they have now corrected my name and are refunding the £25 transfer fee. Sadly, it arrived after the bank had closed.

LJS took us to what we had once referred to as our dream home in Talpe. We liked the landlord, if not what he had done to his house. Now the unpleasant task of informing him we were no longer interested. I shrank from the task and stayed in the car while LJS and Michael went to him. He was charming and asked where I was. I came out of hiding and was very happy there were no ill feelings. He gave us the letter from the bank. I rather think he was enjoying redoing everything and was happy not to have to rush things on our behalf. We later learned he was considering putting in a swimming pool. Unless we could have turned it into a fish pond, we would have really hated it. The front was still a mess and after the heavy rain shower, very muddy underfoot.

With the letter going to that address, it was brought home to us that we had given that address for visa, health insurance, and bank; another complication to sort out.

LJS tells us he has a strimmer and would have the grass cut in our future home. He was very kind and had done so much for us; it's hard to say how we would have managed without his help. We did get a bit concerned over some of his ways that appear odd to us, but no doubt we appear a little odd to him. We both hoped he would not try to run our lives once we settled in. Though he has a business, it does not seem to take up much of his time. We had put our foot down on some of his ideas, such as in the land of the new house, there is, for some reason, a slab of concrete in the grass. He says we can build a hut on it for sitting and drinking beer!

The house does not have an internet connection, but our friend showed us a dongle he has to plug in, which will help us get one.

Tuesday 18th March started as some days before by going to the bank now expecting all was well with my transfer. LJS said he would meet us at the bank or phone. The bank still had not received anything from the UK and told me to email again. We left. We bought a bin to wash clothes in, a wooden spoon, and some sponges. With still no word from LJS, we headed back to Beach Haven. Michael then tried phoning LJS several times without luck. Hours later he got through. LJS was less than pleased with us. He had been phoning, then gone to Beach Haven to be told we had gone to the bank, he went there to find we had left, and kept phoning. He had arranged for us to meet the landlady or mother of the owner and her brother at the office of a lawyer. Somehow the phone had got switched on to silent. Poor man, no wonder he was a bit upset. All was not lost, however; life here was taken at a slower pace and we learned that no one ever expected people to be on time. We met and felt at ease at once with our new landlady. We apologised for the delay and the fact that I still had not received the money I was having transferred. Never mind, she had heard the story and said without being asked that we could move into the house that evening. I could have hugged her. First though, we had to pay one month's rent, back to the bank with LJS, the landlady, brother, and all, where LJS managed to make them release the amount from Michael's account. All smiles, we now went on a shopping spree. Our landlady was very generous, willing to buy us a new fridge, burners, fans, etc. LJS led us to a large shop. Thinking we were going to have to buy the same, we had already found the best deals in another shop and finally it was agreed we would go there. Most hobs had just two burners, but we had found one with a small third suitable for our small coffee pot. Added to that was a very nice eco-fridge, a whistling kettle, and a big water purifier. Floor-standing fans and then on to get new mattresses. LJS kept fingering pillows. "These are good quality," he said, "Ask her to buy some." We told him we had ours and saw no point in making the landlady buy things that we did not really need. "What if Michael and I get drunk on arrack one night and I have to stay over?" I made no reply and made sure he did not get her to buy them. After arranging for everything to be delivered later that day, we made our way back to Beach Haven. Sita was very surprised to learn that everything had happened so fast. My birthday was the following day; knowing this, they had a beautiful birthday cake for me. They gave it to me, and I felt mean that I would not be able to share it with them.

With LJS and a friend, we bought vegetables, rice, etc. for a pre-birthday party in our new home. In the kitchen, I found that their way of making curry and dhal differed from the Indian way. I would buy whole spices, pound them, and fry them. Here in Sri Lanka, the dhal has the same ingredients plus coconut milk, and all the spices are pre-ground. I measured out some dhal; laughter followed. "That is far too much; we have rice and dhal, not dhal and rice." It took a second to take that in. I had always made a large helping of dhal to keep some for the following day when it tastes even better. We left things cooking to have a beer, and Bandusena came in to say the rice was burning and took over. I ignored the suggestion that I could take cooking lessons.

I cut the cake, and we all had a piece. Giving a slice to Bandusena, LJS spoke to him and then told us he had instructed him to treat us as if we were his brother and sister. Very odd.

Chapter Fourteen

A Home at Last

I was awake, and my long-held dream was now real. I was 77 and where I wanted to be, with a house and a huge expanse of land just waiting to be tamed. "HAPPY BIRTHDAY," Michael called as I came out of the bedroom and handed me a watch and a card from Tiverton, the town in the UK we had lived in, by an artist we liked.

I received another phone call from the bank here. They were still asking for my name to be confirmed. Another request was sent to the bank in the UK.

LJS arrived, telling us we had to go to the lawyer before noon. A nice female lawyer with an office in the Fort. She looked at our passport and noted my date of birth, wished me Happy Birthday, and asked us to come again on Monday. We agreed to rent, not lease, the house and then would not have to pay 15%. No one could satisfactorily explain the difference between leasing and renting.

Another visit to the bank, who still had heard nothing. LJS again took charge of things, saying we needed more essentials.

We bought electric energy-saving light bulbs, a mop, and a bucket. Also, switches we did not know we needed but were told they would come in handy.

Later, I returned to the bank and this time saw the manager. We both had to have ten thousand pounds fixed deposit. Michael was able to pay mine. In the end, reason prevailed. They had the money and could see where the mistake lay in the names. I got my account. This now enabled me, like Michael, to get my visa.

Dream Home, we learned, translated to 'Sihina Niwasa'. We added that to our address of Manawila, Walahanduwa. LJS was in a nice mood and said he would make us a mailbox with that name on. A nice thought that came to nothing. We had paid for the eco bulbs, which we thought would give us the right to choose where we wanted them. Not so, LJS decided. That was OK as we intended in the future to change them all, but he insisted that one had to go on the top of a tall pole in the garden. We are against artificial light outside, but there was no stopping him. A huge wooden platform from one of the barns was put against the pole and the bulb was changed. We never, ever switched it on.

After they left, we heaved a sigh of relief at last being alone and went out to the kitchen for some food and coffee. Bandusena had locked the kitchen area.

Next day, while longing to get going on the garden, we still had to get our visa. With just a banana for breakfast, we crossed the road and Bandusana flagged down the bus to Galle. Within 15 minutes, we were at the train station, too early for the seven ten train to Colombo.

Immigration was in no hurry. When our number was called, we were told all our papers were now in order, but we had to pay cash. Back down to the lower floor and changed our money; on our return, our man had vanished. When he did reappear, he told us to wait another ten minutes. They have very long ten minutes in Sri Lanka. Much later, we were able to exchange our receipt for the money paid for the return of our passport. We had a two-year renewable visa! Rather surprised to find the visa was just a small square stamp, not so easy to find in the pages among other full-page brightly coloured visas for shorter stays and less money.

Our man had disappeared. When he finally appeared on the scene, he told us to wait ten minutes. They have very long ten minutes in Sri Lanka. Much later, we handed over our receipt for the money and received back our passport. We had a two- year renewable visa. The visa was just a small square stamp, not easy to find in the pages among other full-page brightly coloured visas for shorter stays and less money, but felt it was a wise move on this government's part not to waste time and money on a flashy visa like some poorer countries.

LJS had joined us and said he would take us to the bus station to get an express bus back to Galle. We were hungry and longed for some fruit and said we preferred to go by train. This fell on deaf ears. We went to a rice and curry place; if we had to travel by bus, we would prefer not to eat first but were given no option. We hate wasting food but left half and then on to the bus. He gave us advice and direction many times on things we were now well aware of. We by this time felt tired, sick, and cold. The immigration had been cold and now the bus was even colder. Then the rain tipped down. The bus was new but not waterproof. Mini waterfalls were running down the rocks along the roadside. We alighted at the first turning after leaving the highway. A short walk to our house had become much longer, and we were soaked to the skin by the time we reached our new home.

A change of clothes and a nap, the rain stopped, and I was finally able to arm myself with some secateurs to cut dead bits and strangling vines off some of the shrubs, uncovering two wonderful large plants belonging to the ginger family. We opened all the doors, did some washing, and a line was put up by Bandusena, who then pointed out to us a very fine lizard clinging to the rain chains. My first wildlife photo in the new house.

The lizard was gone the next morning but returned in the evening. We spent another few hours at the bank getting cheque books, visa cards, etc. The Sterling we had brought in the bank was said to be best changed into rupees, which would give us interest. A bit odd as we thought it had to be Sterling changed into rupees each month for a rupee account. We then had a savings account plus a current account, and the amount we had to have put in the current account each month would come out of the savings. All a bit roundabout, but we felt they knew best and went along with it. We were hours in the bank as we also had to write letters to the bank manager, even though they had all the forms.

The packers inform us that our goods have now been shipped off to Southampton. I have a bad cold. So far, we have had no bread. Our bread making machine is in the container. A Tuk-tuk regularly comes round with bread for sale, playing a tune, but we miss him every time. Michael was getting desperate. He tries to catch him, always failing. That evening we heard the bread man's tune, and Michael ran. "Can't find my shirt," he called. I was not sure why that mattered. He rushed off, and that time he caught him. We had bread, a white loaf, the only kind they had.

The garden was calling loud and clear. I resented every little interruption: paperwork, emails, uninvited visitors. I had seen a few kapok seeds floating past and beat my way through the undergrowth. Progress was slow until I fell down a slope and found myself among coffee bushes and more kapok seeds. Looking up, I found the tree. Later, I realised we could see the top of the tree from our patio. Many months later, the monkeys also found it and were easy to watch among the almost bare branches against the sky.

Bandusena used LJS's strimmer to cut the grass in front of the house. Several large trees grew in the grass, and to my delight, one was a sapodilla, *Achras sapota*. A soft, very sweet round fruit from South America. I loved the fruit when ripe and in the past made necklaces from the shiny black seeds. While the sapodilla did bear fruit, we never once succeeded in getting a ripe one. They remained hard, and the monkeys ate them. We had better luck with two jambu trees. One bearing the familiar crimson red flowers like little powder puffs that would carpet the ground below as they fell, later producing the red fruit with a texture like a woolly apple. More enjoyable to our mind when made into a drink. Its cousin had light yellow flowers and fruit to match. To our surprise, it also produced an abundance of fruit. Surprise, as we thought the palm squirrels were destroying all the flowers. We now think they were partaking of the nectar and by doing so fertilizing the fruit. We loved these happy little palm squirrels that were always around, climbing trees and running like tightrope walkers, along the electric wires.

Another tree in that area I never did discover its name. We were told it had very highly scented flowers. It grew very tall, and if it did have scented flowers, our power of smell must have diminished.

Around the Sapodilla tree were growing ferns among the grass and weeds. Once all the grass and other unwanted plants were removed, the ferns spread and made a feature around the base of the tree. A less obvious and thrilling find was a man-made concrete pond by the red Jambu tree. The water tap was not hard to find; then the edge of the pond, shaped like a clover leaf, became clear. It was filled in with soil. Bandusena set to with us to dig all the soil out. The first find was a scorpion, and then a new, to us, creature doing its best to wiggle back into the earth: a Toeless Snake Skink.

Bandusena did a good job of trying to repair the cracks in the pond, but it still would not hold water for long. We had a professional man, or at least a man who understood cement, redo the whole pond, which was soon full of fish.

All this was just a small part of the land near the house and relatively tidy. For the most part, we needed a machete to cut our way through vines we called trip wires, as they spread everywhere along the ground and over every tree and bush in their way. A friend wrote and asked how long it took to walk round the property, or plantation as it was called. We had no idea; we had yet to find the edge.

We also had friends inside the house. One bathroom had 14 kinds of insects one night. Geckos decorated the walls, feeding on unsuspecting insects. Our favourite beetles were the fireflies. Never many, but usually one would fly around the living area, and it was unusual if I did not have a little light flitting around my bedroom.

Had we found our paradise? Almost, but not quite. The house was situated high above the road and further back. It was not a main road, but the noise of the traffic carried up. Buses not only had noisy engines but honked their horns as they went round the bend. Tuk-tuks, cars, and motorbikes; it was one continuous loud noise during the day. Why we had not noticed it on our visits seemed odd. Perhaps we were too overcome at finding such a perfect place.

Then there was LJS. The man we had so much to be thankful for. He could be as charming as he was when we first met. Now the more we knew him, doubts entered our minds. We were not so comfortable in his company. His behaviour was often offensive or difficult to understand. One morning, he marched in, straight to the kitchen. I followed. He opened the fridge and looked in. "What do you want? Are you looking for something?" I inquired, trying to keep calm. No reply as he went on opening every cupboard. He removed something from a shelf and placed it in a cupboard. He then opened cupboards under the dresser where I had plastic bags I was using to wrap items we did not need and put in a store room. LJS called for Bandusena and had him gather up all the bags and stuff into one. I felt myself boiling over, so I left and climbed up to the grounds above the house, waiting until he left. The next day when he visited, Michael said to him, "You know you upset Angela going through the kitchen." No answer. He went into the room we called the office and then through the adjoining door into my bedroom. His visits in the evening would be to drink our beer and phone one or two of his friends to join him. We would then be regaled with horror stories of things that happened to foreigners who put too much trust in local people. We felt we had done just that by trusting him. He told us we did not understand the ways of people here and we should trust no one. I had made the mistake of letting him use my laptop. From then on, he and his friend would come in, and without a word, go to the office and use my laptop as if it were their property.

So why did we not put our foot down? First, because we did feel indebted to him, and second, we had named him as the person to clear our shipment.

After one week had elapsed, our money was all sorted out at the bank and our landlady was ready to have us pay two years' rent to the lawyers. Again, she arrived with her brother. LJS also came, and this time we were impressed. He behaved well and backed us when we said we would rather just sign for one year, as suggested by Lalith, explaining that we were finding it very noisy.

We all went to the lawyer's office to sign a contract. At one point, the lawyer asked for Rs500. Michael paid. We were all around the desk. As we left, the brother said we should get familiar with the money. I was surprised as I thought we understood it well and said so. He then told me Michael had handed over Rs5,000. When asked for Rs500, his sister and LJS all agreed that he had. Amazingly, none of them had said a word at the time, and the lawyer had taken it. How easy it would have been for one of them to say, "Michael, do you not have a smaller note," or something of that nature. After we had been to the bank and had the money transferred, Michael and I went back to the lawyer. She had gone, so we explained what had happened to another female lawyer, and she got on the phone, went to our lawyer's desk, and took out Rs. 4,500, the change we should have had, and handed it to us with a smile. I was beginning to feel a bit like Alice in Wonderland, where nothing was what it seemed to be.

Myna

Parakeet

Brown headed Barbet

Chapter Fifteen

Feathered Friends

The sun was shining, and we found numerous birds were happy to partake of the of watermelon, pawpaw, banana, mango, any fruit we had put out on the concrete slab, LJS had suggested building a beer drinking den. We started to know some of the birds personally.

There were a number of mynas, usually they came in pairs. One pair, one had a bit of white on its wing, reminding me of a black bird with a bit of white in the UK. They never flew directly to the banquet. They would fly down to that part of the grass and then, in a hurried walk, race to the food. By that time, another pair might have come from the opposite direction. Red-vented Bulbuls were attractive and regular customers. The yellow-billed Babblers came in small groups; they were soft-looking birds that appeared disinclined to fly further than necessary. They would hop along and very often, would be in the company of a palm squirrel. Quite what the attraction was between the bird and mammal was, we could not decide. The strange thing was that very often, without the aid of binoculars or spectacles, we invariably mistook a palm squirrel for a babbler or vice versa. That they were friends, there was no doubt, but the squirrel usually got the lion's share of the fruit they were both after. The big excitement was the first time we saw a Brown-headed Barbet. He was a big fellow compared to the other diners. Yellow around the eye and a brownish-red large bill with a green back and lower half. He or she was an outstanding bird we had not expected to favour us with its appearance. Its size made it greedy, taking large pieces of fruit. On the odd occasion, two came and just once a third. Was it a family? Was the third the pair's chick? They all looked the same. Surprisingly, a Red-backed woodpecker would now and then join in the feast. They, we knew, nested in holes in a group of dead coconut palms in the area above the house.

There were well over 100 coconut palms and a number of fruit trees, all grown to a large size that in some cases we could never get the fruit. One was a huge Rambutan tree. I love the fruit, but all we ever got was the seeds and the bright red rind. Bats and birds had a field day when it was in fruit.

Black and white Magpie Robins liked to watch us do any planting or digging. Flying down as soon as we unearthed a tasty, to them, looking grub, large white beetle grubs were the prized food and were also the favourite of the white-throated kingfisher. The Kingfisher would also hang around when it spotted us digging. But the Magpie Robin and Kingfisher did not compete. We had the company of only one or the other when gardening.

The kingfishers liked to nest in holes in the earth bank on one side of the house. While mostly overgrown, this bank had a number of holes that were home to several species. Often, several birds used some of the many holes. One day, I found a baby kingfisher on the ground looking more than a little bewildered. Either it had fallen out of its hole or been told it was time to fly by its parents and got scared and dropped to the ground. No other kingfisher was around. I gently tossed it in the air while bending down, it landed by my feet. I knew two holes that Kingfishers had been coming out of so placed it by one where there was a shrub it could lean against. I watched from the kitchen window. It did try to fly, but again was back on the ground. Meanwhile, I saw an adult kingfisher near the other hole. I went out and picked up the chick and put it on the ground below that hole. I made my way back. From the window, I found I could not see it. Going back out, I now saw it had gone. Hopefully, it had learned to fly.

Baby kingfisher did not wish to fly.

These Kingfishers, with their iridescent blue plumage, were a delight to see but were also very bossy, noisy birds. I spent hours one day watching a female land monitor lizard enlarging a hole in the bank, laboriously digging, her long body slowly disappearing into the hole. A kingfisher spotted her and kept flying low over her, shrieking its head off, making me at first think the monitor must be after bird eggs. I soon realised as she dug out the soil she was making her nest. I had hopes of seeing the babies emerge one day. I must have missed the big event, but we found later many other wee monitors. Termite nests appeared to be their favoured nesting places. I loved these miniature, prehistoric-looking little creatures.

Monitor Lizard digging a hole in the bank to lay her eggs.

Baby monitor coming out of termite nest

We often saw Black Drongos with their distinctive forked tail, usually sitting on the electric wires.

Then diving after some small insect. One evening, the Drongos and Red-vented Bulbuls appeared to be having a party. A number of both birds were flying around madly and exercising their vocal cords to the full. The air must have been full of flying insects. Until then, I had taken it for granted that the Bulbuls were just fruit eaters. One bird I longed to see was the Indian Paradise Flycatcher, that we had a quick glimpse of in our friend's garden in Bentota. I was rewarded one day when, its undulating long white tail caught my eye as it floated past. It's a little bird that looks as if it was once all white but had had its head dipped in black dye. With a few black traces on its wings. Its tail was about three times the length of its body, just thin streamers. After that, for a few months, we saw it almost daily.

On occasions, we would see a huddle of peahens come up the bank. All we got from their dandy-looking, his spouse was his voice.

The real jewels were the sunbirds. We had both the Purple-rumped Sunbird and the Long-billed Sunbird with its long-curved bill. Their tiny metallic bodies as they flitted among the flowers in our hanging baskets were Asia's answer to America's hummingbirds. Almost too fantastic to take in. It would be hard to be sad or cross while watching these tiny birds.

One day, I found a tree with white flowers that was familiar but could not place just why I felt I knew it. Days passed, and the next time I saw it, I gasped. Now full of bright red fruit, I knew it as a West Indian cherry, full of vitamin C. Often in the West Indies, hotels would have them in the grounds as they were so decorative.

Shame ours was not in a better position. The Green Imperial Pigeons knew all about it, and as they gorged themselves, made the tree even more spectacular. I had viewed it from below and now made a path through very overgrown ground to clear around its base. The ground was covered with berries, many not having been pecked at, and I could reach some still on the tree without depriving the pigeons. The fruit is not as tasty to eat raw as a true cherry and has three small seeds, but it makes perfect jelly; the clear red jelly in a glass jar looks as good as it tastes. The Imperial Pigeon is the largest of the pigeon and Dove families, found in Sri Lanka with a striking appearance. The small Emerald Dove is a delightful little dove. A pair would often be seen on the grass, walking around nodding their heads as if in approval at the seeds they might be finding on the ground.

A Spotted dove always looked very elegant, slender with an upright pose. A pair made their nest in the rafters of an outbuilding we had. We watched the progress and looked forward to seeing the chicks. It was not to be. One day we found the nest and two lifeless chicks on the ground. Careless parents or, more likely, a snake, rat, or palm civet had knocked down the nest. Perhaps even a large fruit bat, a flying fox. These bats would soil the walls, leaving seeds taken from the jak fruit on the ground.

The Oriental Turtle Dove looked much more robust, and pairs were forever courting around the outside of the house.

Sometimes we would only catch a glimpse of a bird and not be sure just what we had seen. If Bandusena was with us and had seen it, he would know, and a search through the bird book would take place so he could show us what we had seen.

The Greater Coucal, a large bird, was very obliging and would stay more or less in the same spot for some time while we stood admiring it. The first time we saw an Asian Koel, we had no idea what we were looking at and turned to the book. It was a female, beautifully spotted and barred in black and white. We thought far smarter than her more crow-like black husband.

One of the first trails we cleared was up to the back of the house. Here, we were behind the house, which cut out the noise of the traffic. Having cleared a path, Bandusena produced a garden seat. This was our favourite place at the end of the day to sit, share a beer, and watch the birds. Here, there were mostly coconut palms. What a wonderful palm it is; every bit has a use as well as being decorative and bending at different angles. It was the few dead but still standing palms that proved the most interesting. These had been turned into multi-racial high-rise apartments. Parakeets, mynas, barbets, and, of course, the woodpeckers were all happily competing to find the best nesting hole. Then flocks of parakeets would take off. We hardly ever saw them lower down at house level or even on the other side of the plantation. Egrets would take off as the sun sank lower, from the paddy field turning from silver to black as they wheeled across the sky. Our seat had been placed with its back to a cashew tree. Rather, it was a branch of the tree that lay parallel, almost at ground level but still retained life. The cashew fruit appeared, the nut hanging down from it. We had only a few, and those were not fully ripe within days; that, and our other cashew trees had been stripped of their fruit. Bats? Birds? We never knew. Bandusena, seeing how we enjoyed that spot, then constructed a table, and later we slung a hammock between the palms. This was our spot, and LJS and friends were not invited.

As we cleared more ground and unwrapped bushes and trees from their covering of vines of many kinds, we discovered it was not just palms, cinnamon, and cashews. There was one pretty tree that the birds loved on the edge of the top of the bank. At times, it was covered in berries. Berries that Bandusena indicated were not for humans. The birds took advantage and loved them. Banana plants grew among the cassava. The fruit of the banana had to be covered to stop the monkeys taking them while green. The cassava plants, like the young Pawpaw trees, stood little chance against the porcupines. It is my regret that we never saw the porcupines, only its tracks, the damage it had caused and now and then it left us, as a peace offering, a quill. They are nocturnal and after spending most of the day working on the land, we were so tired we went to bed early. Bandusena saw one and two another night.

Several times, we would hear the cry of a raptor. Michael particularly liked these birds and was more than pleased to see a Changeable Hawk Eagle. With the aid of the book, there was no mistaking this Eagle. For he obligingly would choose an open and clearly visible place, usually a dead branch we could see from the house; his crest and fancy little topknot was his signature. Why he was called changeable was a mystery he kept to himself. To us, he always looked the same.

Changeable Hawk Eagle

Magpie Robin

Greater Coucal

Chapter Sixteen

The Arrival of Our Container

LJS still remained, when he was not in Colombo, treating the place as if he owned it. Time for the arrival of our container was getting close, and he told us it would arrive some days early. I checked online and found it would be in Singapore on the date he mentioned. We were getting very worried that we had named him as our agent to release our goods. Now, I wondered if he had any idea what it all involved. The date given for our container of goods to arrive in Colombo came, and I checked. I found a phone number and spoke to a man who said yes, it had arrived and was being offloaded, and we could come and do the paperwork. How I wished we were doing it ourselves, but it was now made out to LJS. I phoned him to suggest we leave straight away and meet him in Colombo. He did not answer. He always had his phone in his hand. Why, I wondered, would he not answer? To our relief, he drove up our drive. His charming smile had been replaced with a very worried tired look.

I then expected he would take us to Colombo in his car as he had stressed we would have to be there personally. When I suggested we had better get going, he said the container had not arrived. I told him I had spoken to a man who assured me it had. "Who did you talk to?" he demanded more than asked. I did not know the name of the person. Slumping down on the patio, he gave in and said yes, it had arrived but it was not a good day to clear it as it would take more than one day, and then it would be the weekend, and they would charge us for storage. This we felt was crazy, but there was no shifting him. Either he was worried he had bitten off more than he could chew or had had a heavy night before, drinking. He then got back in his car and went to sleep.

Some days prior to this, drinking our beer with his friend, they had talked together in English for a change, saying how they could get the coconuts picked and share the profit. I heard but took it to be the beer talking. I did butt in to say we already had two people interested in buying the coconuts. Someone else was going to find a picker for us. No more was said.

We had to comply with his idea that it was best to go on Monday to Colombo. We felt more than worried as we also felt that surely we would have to pay for the storage.

Sunday morning, Bandusena came to us and said, "Coconuts." Why, we were not sure, but went out and saw a man climbing one of the palms. Odd, but perhaps he had found a picker or our friend had sent him. We then got busy moving all the furniture out of the living area so all our boxes could be brought in the following day, as we hoped. To our surprise, LJS's friend arrived looking less than happy, sat down, and made numerous phone calls. He had no time to talk to us or help in any way. When he left, he was replaced by another friend, one we were to call Manny, who turned into a true friend. He sat up in our bird-watching place and said LJS had told him to be there, but why he did not know. Days later, we learned the truth. LJS decided to carry out his plan to rob us of the coconuts and had arranged a picker, and his friend had to try and find buyers. Apparently, a task he did not find easy. In the days we were in Colombo, the coconuts that had been picked all vanished except some Bandusena had kept back for our use. We lost out, but the laugh was, we were told later they had to dispose of them at a very low price and had made next to nothing.

It was wishful thinking that we might get our container on Monday. Monday, Tuesday, and Wednesday were the most stressful days. LJS had gone to Colombo and told us to get a train and meet him. We did and were dragged around from office to office, trying, so he said, to find a man who would discharge it cheaply. The first morning we arrived in Colombo tired and hungry. He took us to an office and in English told a man he had to bring us with him as we did not trust him or believe he knew what he was doing, etc. Now he said he felt like committing suicide. In return, the man said nothing. This was another change of personality. We were amazed as we had not said we did not trust him and had signed papers giving him full authority to act on our behalf. We had not wanted to travel to Colombo personally. In the past, I had moved crates of belongings from one country to another, often without even being in the country. Here LJS told us it did not work like that. He also said we should have put the shipment in both our names, not just mine; the shipper in the UK had told us otherwise.

If anything was actually achieved that first day, we were unaware of it. Finally, at his insistence, we returned to Galle on the new Express bus, which made us feel sick and cold; it was so air-conditioned that when it rained, we got wet. The next two days were much the same, except we were dishing out money for various things, including storage for the preceding days. At one point, we sat parked in the dock area, a place quite unrecognisable from my first encounter so many years before. Then a motorcycle pulled up. LJS talked to him and then asked to see my passport. Taking it, he handed it over to the driver who drove off! This could not be happening; surely I was having a nightmare. I was awake, but there was nothing I could do about it.

The third day was all day, racing around from one place to another. Ending up at a place we had been to on the first day where the man asked why he had not agreed to use him on Monday. LJS's reply was, "I was doing them a good turn and trying to find someone cheaper." We had, as instructed, a large amount of cash and were handing it out like visiting cards. We now paid this man who was sympathetic to us. My bag was still open. LJS says, "Give him a tip," and extracts a note and then another, handing them to the man who looked puzzled as if he did not know what to do. They had a baby bird in the office, rescued from a cat, which I was given to try and make well. Why we could not then have returned, we did not know, but we did have lunch at a Buddhist place I had seen passing. It was a perfect peaceful place with, of course, vegetarian food. Here LJS was back to his charming ways, but not for long. On the way back, he asked to borrow two thousand rupees. I just said, "later." We stopped at one point, and he got out and returned with a bottle wrapped in newspaper. No prize for guessing what that was. He told us he had got a big commission for getting us the house but was not telling his wife. Trying to make conversation, I told him that one of the street dogs had produced three puppies in one of the storage rooms on a mattress Bandusena had put down for her. No response. Then suddenly he said that if the landlady knew we let wild dogs in the house, she would commit suicide. I learned later from his friend that he often used the word "suicide." Things did not get better when, for some reason, his new smartphone failed to work. He needed to phone Bandusena to get men to offload the container. That too he had not thought to mention or arrange. At long last, we stopped just before turning off to our place. The container was there, parked and waiting, and were told to follow us. Normally, it would have been exciting to be once again reunited with all our things. We both felt so tired and worn out; all we would have really liked to do was to lie down and sleep. LJS then asked Michael to loan him some money; when asked how much, he said "five thousand". Michael handed it over; we were both like zombies. We had become so used to being asked for money that we just dished it out.

The container managed, to our surprise, to get up the drive. Bandusena found some men and he and they set to offloading. LJS phoned his friend, and they sat outside drinking, then calling a halt to the offloading and getting the men to buy more arrack with thousands of rupees he had made us part with to give to the men as now they were his friends joining him in drinking until the bottles were empty. Bandusena too was included in the party, but he also carried in things when the others stopped. I was trying to keep account of the number of boxes, etc., but some were going in one room and others in the main room. At long last, the container was empty and left.

LJS told Michael to come out and join in the drinking. I do not think we would have had the energy to lift a glass. We went into the kitchen and brewed some coffee. Bandusena came, a little tipsy but understanding how tired we were. He fried us up some berries and jak nuts; these were more than welcome. We said good night, closed and locked the doors as we had been told many times by LJS to do. He and his friend stayed outside; we left the light on for them.

Those three days were not happy memories, but the future was. It was many months before we saw or heard of LJS again. Whether it was because he was ashamed of his behaviour or just that he did not wish to return the five thousand, we were not sure, but felt the price was worth it to have the place to ourselves. We heard that he told his friends we were rude, that after we had got all our stuff inside, we had locked the doors and refused to drink with him. True, BUT...

We enjoyed the company of LJS's friend, whom we called Manny, when he came alone. Over time, Manny became a good and true friend. After some months, in conversation with Manny, I mentioned knowing Don Windsor years ago in Galle. Don was Manny's uncle!

fair, they would often leave us a gift of a quill which I liked to keep, and the dogs liked to chew, in the same way they liked chewing on large feathers.

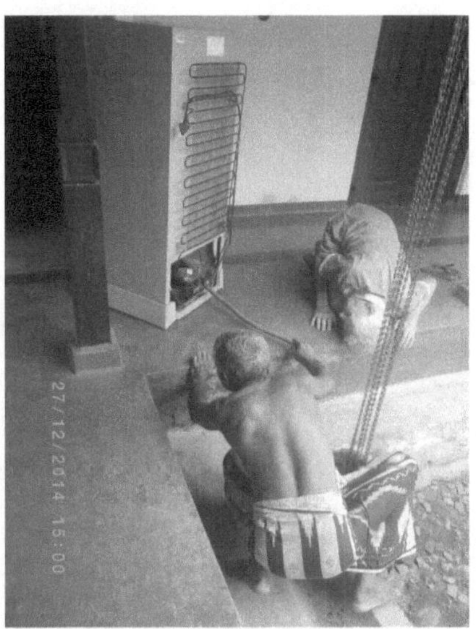

Snake Hunt

Young Palm Civet

Palm Squirrel kisses plant holder

Chapter Eighteen

Snakes, Monitors, and Tourist Turtles

The first cobra I found was near the patio and very small. Small, though it was, I had unintentionally disturbed it, and it raised its little body and opened its hood before getting a little scared at its own bravado and vanishing down a hole. I called Michael, who sat next to the hole armed with his camera. Every now and then, the snake would pop its head up, take one look at Michael, and retreat back down.

Later, we were fortunate enough to see full-size cobras several times, always near the house or on the patio. The dogs would bring our attention to them by barking, standing a few feet from the snake that had reared up and opened its hood. After taking several photos and calling the dogs away, the cobra would move off.

There was a bathing pool some distance from the house. NOT a swimming pool. Bathing pools have walls around them for a bit of privacy. They are intended for laundering clothes and washing your body. Ours had steps leading down to it and a paved area to sit, stand, etc. It was filled by a well. We did wonder if it held any aquatic life other than pond skaters. That is until one day we saw a very large water monitor taking a dip with its head above water. The water at that time was rather low. It was easy to see how it could have dropped in but we did wonder how it would get out. We got a log and found the edge was over five feet deep but finally managed to rig up something that it may or may not have used. Naturally, I took a photo and from the photo, I could see a fish. So we had fish which later I added to and fed. That was not all, several times a *water snake would be swimming about but did not appear to be interested in eating the fish. In fact, I would often find it among the fish who paid no heed to it. That is until one day I was feeding the fish who ate and acted as normal.

Suddenly, a carp darted away, went in circles, and acted as if it had gone quite mad. This agonizing death dance went on for some time before I finally saw what was happening. The water snake had Xenochrophis asperrimus part of the fish in its jaws. The carp had put up a good fight, but finally, it was over. The snake very callously came out of the water with half of the lovely big carp hanging out of its mouth, looking very proud of itself. Perhaps it thought I put the fish in for it and was showing its thanks.

I now think the snake, unlike the fish, ate tadpoles. I used to get hundreds of toad tadpoles in the pond near the house. I kept taking them out and putting them in the bathing pool, and by the following day, could see none.

One day, the pond had an overabundance of mating toads. I caught a pair and took them to the bathing pool. They carried on as if nothing had disturbed them. Catching another pair, I returned to release them in the same pool. My original pair were struggling in the jaws of a water snake. I say pair, but it was the female who had been caught by the leg and was trying to climb up the bank, and the snake was trying just as hard to drag her into his hole. Her small husband, still attached to her back, blissfully unaware of his lover's predicament or so it appeared. At first, only the front end of the snake was out of its hole; now it came further out trying to get a better grip on the toad, which was sometimes upside down or under the water but still put up a good fight. The second couple, who I had dropped in the pool, often passed the ongoing fight but took no notice. What, I wondered, did the male think? His mate, who had once been so willing, had somehow flown to another pool of water and was thrashing around in a most unladylike manner. If she was still producing a string of sperm, it was not possible to see. Several times I thought the female toad had died as she was still, but she was just catching her breath for another struggle. Finally, the male, after what he must have considered a very uncooperative mate, hopped off, climbed out of the water, and made for the paddy field. This was just what the snake needed. His jaws could not open wide enough to get around the bodies of the two of them. With the male gone, the snake was able to pull more of the female into its mouth. The end was close; only the head and front legs stuck out of its assailant's mouth, it no longer moved. I felt bad about taking the toad to its death; on the other hand, even a snake has to eat. I could have wished that death had not taken two hours. I left the pool and returned a few hours later; the snake now lay in the water, a bulge showing how far down the toad had gone. It looked rather uncomfortable, exhaustion, or indigestion?

A toad is a bit of a mouthful for this water snake

We rather doubted Bandusena when he picked up a wooden ornament of a turtle and spread his hands to indicate one about a foot long. Indicating that we had two. We followed him down to the pool. No surprise, no giant turtles. No more was said on the subject, but a few nights later, Michael was woken by tapping on his window. Bandusena was holding up a large pond turtle.

I was woken, and we admired what I would have called a large terrapin. The books now call it a pond turtle. It, also according to the local books, was only found in the North of the country. Perhaps this one was a tourist. It would have been too far in the dark to take it down to the bathing pool to see if it would like to go in, so we placed it in a large cement tank in the yard for the night. Even Bandusena had misjudged its climbing abilities. In the morning, it was gone. A much smaller one found its own way to the bathing pool and stayed for a short while.

Even with the help of books on the subject, we were finding it difficult to identify all the snakes we found. Bandusena might have a local name for them, but he, also hunting through the book, would not be sure. A nice yellow snake we finally decided, probably wrongly, was a Buff-striped Keelback.

Sri Lanka is well known for the large number of snakes it has. This is probably due to the fact that unlike many countries, where, if someone sees a snake, regardless of whether it is poisonous or not, they kill it. I have not heard or witnessed anyone killing a snake in Sri Lanka.

I was amazed one day when Bandusena, smiling, handed me an arrack bottle containing not the hard liquor it proclaimed on its label but a live Russell's viper. As he well knew, a very poisonous snake. Just how he had managed to get it into the bottle, we never knew. Playing it safe, we took a photo of it while still in the bottle. Later, Bandusena took it off to release it away from the property so the dogs would not get bitten.

Many happy hours were spent watching various kinds of lizards. They did not mind being stared at and could sit in one place for a long time. For the most part, they are brown, but sometimes you manage to spot a bright green one, outstanding in its colourful coat but easily overlooked in the green vegetation. When courting, the male does his best to seduce his love with a brilliant display of colour. Courting goes on for ages, and we have yet to see the final act. Perhaps they wait for us to go.

Digging in the garden often brought surprises. Once, something I first took to be another toeless snake skink was turned up. But this one had a head like a hammer. I thought it might be a shark-headed snake skink, but could not find a picture of it, and the shark-headed species is reported to only be found in the dry northwest of the country. This chap was in the wet southwest.

Snail shells, like the African giant snail but not quite as large, were not uncommon. All were empty. We only saw two with someone at home. Both times they were found sliding up a wall. Slugs, too, were a rare sight. All we found were small and none on any vegetation, with the exception of one found on a dead leaf.

A couple of times, we found scorpions in the leaf litter. By drawing a circle around them, it assured that they stayed put while we went for the camera.

Few frogs were found, but toads were numerous. I think they have few enemies other than snakes. Like other things, I doubt if anyone kills amphibians of any kind, but not everyone enjoys seeing them. Some are considered lucky; others, toads in particular, and tree frogs are considered poisonous. We noticed that even the dogs, who investigate most things, leave toads alone, supposedly due to the poison of their skin. Snakes, however, will swallow a toad whole.

When we first had the pond near the house repaired and filled with water, I was amazed to find the very next morning, tadpoles were in the water. Surely, I thought spawn could not have come out of the tap, the water of which came from a well and was our drinking water. Then I saw attached to the side of the pond a white mass. A large jambu tree grew next to the pond and towered above it. A tree frog had dropped its offspring in a foam nest into the water. These were nice little tadpoles or "dingoes" – the delightful, easy-to-pronounce and remember Sinhala name. We only saw them leave as frogs by chance, when we shone a light into the pond and witnessed the wee frogs hop off the weed and onto the bank, taking advantage of the night to conceal their leaving.

Many months later, I saw tree frog spawn on the large leaf of a spider lily over hanging the pond. On closer inspection, I saw a water snake entwined in the spawn, gorging itself on tadpoles about to drop in the water. I was able to save quite a number and brought them up in a tank in the courtyard. They all finally grew legs and hopped off, often still showing some tail.

Chapter Nineteen

Addopted by Dogs

When we moved to Sri Lanka, we had made the decision not to have any pets. This was in part because there were still places in Sri Lanka we had not yet visited and wished to be free to do so. The other, of course, was our age. Michael is in his early seventies and I am in my late seventies. It seemed far better that any pet would outlast us, than what would happen.

I should have known that any such decision was not ours to make. I have had numerous pets in the past, but all of them have come to me of their own accord or been given to me as unwanted pets.

No dog actually came with our house in Walahanduwa. However, I had seen how the little mangy dog with a clipped ear followed Bandusena around, and also a Black female. Fair's fair, and they were here first. Though shy of coming in the house, I took it for granted it was where they would like to be.

Our friend Manny suggested that the dog should go to the vet and have its mange treated. He discussed it was with Bandusena, who must have agreed. Manny had a car, so he, Bandusena, and Hyena took off for an animal clinic. They returned with a medical book, showing the date for her next appointment. Manny then flew off for medical treatment in India. From the medical book, we learned her name was Rosi, later we added an "e". One treatment was not enough, so for subsequent treatments, I accompanied Bandusena and Rosie in a tuk-tuk, the driver being a relation of Bandusena. It was a charity clinic run by a German lady, a much-needed clinic as we found out. They treated street dogs for free, but when I went, the cost got a little higher each time, hopefully enabling them to treat more street dogs or, as I preferred to call them, "Free Range".

Author with baby Lucy

Blackie with Lucy, Simon and Richard

Rosie a friend to Blackie and good Aunt to the puppies.

Pee Wee Only stayed a short time but lived up to his name

When we first arrived in Sri Lanka to take up residence, I had written to Virginia MaKenna telling her our change of address and remarked about the dogs, saying how sad it was seeing large dogs, often Alsatians with heavy coats, more suited to colder climates, kept in purpose-built cages in people's gardens as guard dogs. While the free range dogs lead a happy, free life. Opposite our house was a large compound and coop building, the local hangout for a lot of dogs, Rosie included. We knew Bandusena fed Rosie, and we often witnessed a man arrive on a bike who would call all the dogs. To us, it sounded as if he was yelling at them, but the dogs knew and came to accept a square of newspaper on which was deposited a large mound of rice, mixed with curry, etc. Each dog having its own portion. We suspected he got it from leftovers at a restaurant. At first glance, it all looked like a happy arrangement.

About the same time, Virginia received a letter from Rachel. Rachel had been on holiday in Hikkaduwa and was appalled at the condition of the dogs she saw on the beaches. She, with some other shocked tourists, had taken some to a vet and done what they could. On returning to the UK, Rachel had started a charity to help Hikkaduwa strays. At the time of writing, she has sold her house to raise funds and had over 200 dogs and some cats spayed, vaccinated, and where necessary, wounds treated. Virginia wrote and put Rachel in touch with me. I soon started seeing dogs that badly needed treatment. All dogs without a home get to know where they are best looked after.

Buddhist temples are a favourite. These stray dogs were fortunate, but, by one means or another, dogs usually have someone to feed them; no one thinks of their health needs. The government is only interested in vaccinating for rabies.

Rosie was not the only coop dog to cross the road to our place. On the first morning, after having breakfast on the patio and clearing the table, the top of the butter-like spread container was missing. A black pregnant dog had gone off with it. The next morning, the whole container vanished. Bandusena pointed to the same black dog who was on the grass enjoying a very greasy meal. He indicated if he should tell her off. We said "no". She obviously needed it more than we did.

When it was time for the puppies to be born, unknown to us, Bandusena put a couple of old mattresses in a room off the yard, probably used to dry cinnamon in the past. It was just before we got our shipment that he made the announcement that three pups had been born: two boys and a girl. At first, we had referred to her as the 'black dog'. Now she appeared to be part of the family, so we changed her name to Blackie.

Blackie was not a small, friendly little thing like Rosie. She would not allow us anywhere near her room. Once Michael passed near, and out she came and bit him. Bandusena, on the other hand, went in and brought out two of the pups to show us.

If Blackie had a name before we knew her, no one knew. When I had a treat for her, she always responded by coming out of her room, waiting for me to toss her the treat. Refusing at first to take it from my hand. The door to the maternity ward was, of course, always kept open so she could come and go as she wished. One day we all heard Blackie barking in a way we had not heard before. It brought us running to the yard. Here was the reason for her distress. A huge water monitor was along the wall outside her room. Another minute and it would have been inside and made a meal of a puppy. It stopped in its tracks as we all arrived from various directions. I took its photo, and Bandusena made it move along, none too quickly, with the aid of a broom. We watched it go across the grass and down a bank to the road. A week or so later, there was a repeat performance.

As the puppies grew, Blackie allowed them out to play in the yard. During her confinement, she must have missed her friends at the coop compound and would go off in the night to visit, leaving her puppies.

One morning, one puppy was missing. Simon, we searched the grounds, but deep down we had little hope. It was a fair bet that the water monitor had returned and taken its meal.

I had by then given them names based on their tails. Simon was Simon as he had a straight tail, and it was the first name that came to mind, starting with an "S". The other boy had a tail that curled to the right, so he became Richard. The girl had a left-curling tail and was a smart little thing, so she became Lucinda, or Lucy for short.

In town one day, I saw and bought a bag of puppy food. It was put in the traditional kitchen, left for Bandusena to give as required. The puppies only got one meal. Blackie got in and ate the lot. During this time, Rosie would often be in the yard. When the puppies were still in their room, Blackie and Rosie were friends, but Blackie would not let Rosie near the puppies while they were small. Once they were bigger, Blackie became less protective, and finally, she would take them off down the driveway and across the road to join the coop group. The road was usually busy, but both Rosie and Blackie were, like all the free-range dogs, traffic-wise. They would cross the road walking on either side of the two pups. Rosie was a good aunt. Then Richard vanished. This time we suspected someone had taken a fancy to him; male dogs were mostly preferred. We just hoped he had a good home. When mother, Aunt, and Lucy spent more time across the road, I got worried. I did not wish Lucy to be one of many and miss out on injections and bring more puppies into the world. When Lucy had been left in the coop grounds for two days, I was really upset. Michael crossed the road, picked her up, and brought her back to me. From then on, she would never go out of the gate. She loved me, and I her. She was cute, but I never realised what a wonderful little animal I had taken on.

By then, both Blackie and Rosie were spending more time in the house, and we were buying dog food and feeding them. They would still like to cross the road to the compound, and Rosie liked to lie under a parked bus which leaked oil. If it had been Blackie, it would not have been so noticeable, but Rosie was blond. Bandusena often took her under his shower for a wash. She was, as far as we were concerned, really his dog, as was Blackie. One day, Rosie was completely unrecognizable, covered all over in black engine oil. Thinking she needed more than the soap Bandusena used, I handed him some liquid soap and a cloth. I could not believe it when he said a firm "No". We could not leave her like that, but at that time she was not ours, and we had never tried to wash her. She thought the same. When we did grab her and the hose, we became covered in black oil, and she looked just the same. We needed help. I e-mailed Rachel; she recommended talc powder.

We were in luck; a tour of the small local shops produced talc. It said it was for men; they had nothing for lady dogs but figured it would do. Rosie had gone back to the compound. The next day we covered her in talc powder, rubbing it in and brushing it off. It did the trick.

This got Rosie clean, but the mystery remained as to why Bandusena, usually so willing to help and whom we believed loved Rosie and regarded her as his own, had acted the way he did. As time went by, Rosie decided to sleep in our house, as did Blackie. Lucy grew, and from day one, decided my bed was also hers.

We decided when taking Rosie to the clinic that Blackie should be neutered. Our tuk-tuk driver had a little English, and it appeared that Bandusena agreed. I asked if and when it could be done and how much. The amount the clinic wanted for the operation was way more than expected. Both men said no. Later, we found a regular vet who was willing to come to the house and neuter Blackie. A date was set; by now, the dogs hung around us, so we did not expect any difficulty. One of the large tables on the patio was prepared, and all the dogs sat around us. The vet filled his needle to sedate Blackie. As if Blackie had read his thoughts, she suddenly got up and ran off. We had planned to have Lucy spayed at a later date. Before we could fully comprehend what was happening, the vet said he might as well spay Lucy and plunged in the needle. I was in shock; I felt she was too young; I could not bear it. The vet needed an assistant; Michael, like me, was not keen, so Bandusena stepped in. I came inside praying all would be well. When it was all over, they carried the little thing in to me. I held her and then saw Blackie returning as the vet left. I moved into my bedroom and shut the door. Lucy was still unconscious. Blackie sensed where she was and that all was not as it should be. She howled and scratched at the bedroom door. It was a nightmare. When Lucy finally woke, I carried her wrapped in a towel to show Blackie, who, after all that fuss, barely looked at her.

The following week, the vet returned. This time we had Blackie inside. Blackie pulled through as her daughter had done and now was very affectionate to us, perhaps thinking she had had a bad dream.

By then, it had become an accepted fact that all three dogs were part of our family.

Before the last episodes, when the puppies were still confined to their birthplace, Bandusena was working on the flower bed along the drive, and I was nearby. An attractive young, black and white male dog appeared. He called it and, turning to me, smiled and said, "Boy." I was surprised he encouraged it. Bandusena slept in a room on the other side of the yard. He also had a wife and house nearby and would go home for his midday meal. When he left, I expected the dog to follow, but no, he told the dog to stay. I loved the dogs but felt we might be getting overrun with them as, apart from Rosie and Blackie, we often had a male who Bandusena said was Lucy's father. If so, Lucy did not take after either of her parents, being by far the most beautiful. He was not like the others and I do not think he liked us but would walk through the house now and then. After the puppies were big, he stopped even visiting. Then there were the three puppies, and now another, making seven in total. Black & White was a lovely-looking dog, but his manners in the house left a lot to be desired. Apart from taking all the best places to sit or sleep, he lifted his leg and had a wee all over the place. We called him Pee Wee. He was only a lodger as after a few days he left, Bandusena, we think, had found him a home.

As Lucy grew, she developed perfect manners. While the other two enjoyed the comfort of sleeping in the house on the floor, she slept in my bed and in a chair next to me in the evenings. We never taught her anything or trained her; we like a dog to be a dog. However, she loved and still does, holding up her front paw. Not just to shake but to hold. She has never liked strangers, will go out of her way not to get near anyone. Michael, Bandusena and I are her family. We love her and she knows it. Before we retire at night, Bandusena comes in to lock up. We know he is coming in by Lucy's greeting noise. She jumps around him and then back to her chair. As he passes to go out, she sits up and holds out a paw. Of course, he loves her; who could not?

Yes, he loved Lucy, but Rosie then got less attention. Rosie, who had been his and loved him. One day, he was greeting Lucy and patting her, and Rosie came up, wagging her tail. She was ignored. She turned away, tail between her legs. If dogs had tears, I would have seen tears in her eyes. Blackie too got less attention, partly owing to the fact that Lucy demanded it all.

A couple of years later, when we had moved and Bandusena visited about twice a month to cut the grass, all three would give him a rapturous welcome. Lucy regarded him as her own and got the lion's share; the others too received their petting and treats. We were back to being a happy family.

Richard, the puppy with a tail curling to the right, turned up in our garden about a year after he was born. He was much like Lucy, and at first, I thought it was her. He was thinner but had a black ribbon round his neck, so we think someone loved him. He showed little interest in his sister, who wanted to be friends. He would go to Blackie, his mother, who showed little interest. To clinch the matter, he went round the house and into the yard and to the room where he was born. There was no doubt about it. Richard had returned. He often paid short visits, but sadly, Blackie was not friendly to him, and Lucy he ignored. Only Rosie appeared to remember him, but then she is more friendly. Finally, he stopped coming.

Naturally, we played with Lucy, bought balls, etc. This was a local novelty; few people ever played with their dogs. Lucy learned to catch and play with a number of things, and slowly Blackie and Rosy decided it was not too undignified to join in.

Chapter Twenty

Looking for Leopards

Among the many changes since our earlier visits to the country was the amount of traffic that now clogged the roads. To make it worse, there appeared to be no rules governing the way people drove.

A vehicle would come out of a side road to join the main stream of traffic, without so much as a glance to see what was coming. Tuk-tuks would overtake on either side and wind in and out of the traffic.

We were fortunate that it was not necessary to have our own means of transport. Regular buses to Galle stopped outside the coop compound opposite and on our return dropped us at our gate. To get to more specific places, to buy plants, etc., we just had to call the Tuk-tuk we always used. Michael had his fold-up bike, and soon learned that you never assume other drivers will do as you expect. If they indicate they are going to turn, it does not mean they will. On the other hand, they might just turn ahead of you without any signal. He enjoyed his cycle rides into Galle and managed to survive many tricky moments.

With so much to keep us occupied around the house - cutting trails, planting, and enjoying the wildlife - we had not given a thought to our plan to visit other places. That is until Manny suggested that he hire a 4X4 and we, along with his family, go to visit Yala National Park. We had been there once before but had not been lucky enough to see a leopard. This time, also with the palu berries out that sloth bears *Melursus ursinus* love, there would be a good chance to see the bears. Manny assured us we would certainly see a leopard as, using our own hired transport, we could spend as much time as we like in the park looking. This sounded perfect, and so a date was set.

We spent the day getting to the area, stopping on the way and staying the night at Tissa. Manny's family was large, in width rather than numbers. His wife, two big sons, a small daughter, plus another member of the family who would share the driving, totalling eight with us, rather a Tight fit. With the advantage of being far older than anyone else, I had the passenger seat next to the driver. One stop was to see a blow hole, a natural occurrence, but some enterprising person had set up a booth and charged visitors. Rs. 200 is not a lot, £1 each. We offered to pay for the others. Only the children wanted to go, but it was a costly visit. We were told we were foreigners and so had to pay Rs. 2,000 each! Never again. It was a long uphill walk on stone steps. The blow hole was much the same as other blow holes we had visited free of charge in other countries.

Manny being an engineer wanted to show us the new port being built in Hambantota. He felt it was not a good project and was costing the country millions, with the only beneficiaries being the Chinese. It would be a whole new town when finished, and the expectation was that container ships would be happy to use it and bring in more imported cars to clog the roads. For our part, we found it horrendous, hot, dry, and with a gale-force wind. Discharging anything would have some problems. We decided against seeing the new airport, which later was to become a white elephant.

The place we enjoyed the most was the Botanical Gardens. It is hotter and drier in the south, not a place we would choose to live, but plants were different - cacti, Dragon fruit, which we tried to grow in our place and failed. Paw Paw was a surprise; they grow large and in abundance. It is an easy tropical tree to grow, unless you have a porcupine. Why it should prefer the hot and dry area, I had no idea. The most gratifying find was Hibiscus. I had been trying to buy what I expected to be a common bush, but nobody understood the name. I had resorted to a few cuttings I could take when I saw the plant near the roads. Here, the plants were all labelled with their names in English. The Hibiscus was called a "Shoe flower"! No one could tell me why. Being English, it was thought I should know. Some years later, reading R. Raven-Hart's "Ceylon History in Stone", I found the answer. The red flowers are used to polish shoes! As we have no shoes to polish, we have been unable to try it out. Also, the flowers come in a large variety of colours.

We were particularly keen to visit the "Birds Research Centre" in Hambantota. Only Manny joined us. The others wisely said they were not interested. It was another Rs. 2,000 each for Michael and me. Manny told them we were residents and I had my passport to confirm it. They were not interested. Thinking we were going to learn a lot about the local bird life, we felt that this time it would be worth the extra cost.

The wind was like that experienced at the port, doing its best to knock us off our feet. We beat our way from cage to cage. Not a single local bird. The cages were mostly bare of any kind of vegetation, and while some had the name up, it was very sparse on information. They even had ostriches in an open-air pen. In Africa, they race for miles; here reduced to short walks. A very sad place.

We had booked two rooms at the Vikum Lodge in Tissamaharama, where Michael and I had stayed before. Up until then, a few miles from our destination, the traffic had not been a problem. We then hit the biggest traffic jam ever. A two-lane road with everyone going in the same direction became four lanes. Tough if someone had wanted to drive in the opposite direction. The occupants in the various forms of transport looked in a party mood. Everyone was going to the Kataragama Festival. Kataragama is the second most holy place in Sri Lanka, after Adam's Peak. Holy to Buddhists, Hindus, and Muslims alike. Some of the pilgrims walk the length of the island, taking 45 days to reach this holy spot. They were probably moving faster than we were.

At last, we were able to pull away from the traffic and make our way to Vikum Lodge. In our previous visit, the owner had been wanting to sell and had, sadly for us, found a buyer. The new owner was pleasant enough, but how the rooms had managed to deteriorate was hard to imagine. Michael and I shared a room, along with a huge spider and a cockroach or two. Manny and the family were quite happy to all crowd into one room after getting a third single bed put in. Apparently, they pushed them together and all slept in any space available. How wonderfully adaptable people are here. We were only thankful they had not suggested we too join them.

After an early dinner, we piled back into the four by four and set off for Kataragama Festival. About a sixteen-kilometre drive. This was the last day of the festival, a poya day (full moon). Not surprisingly, a few million people had arrived well before us. Every available space one might have parked was already taken. When we were able to park, we had a long walk ahead of us. I felt I was dropping to sleep on my feet; we had put a walking stick in the vehicle in case the need to climb a mountain arose. Now the way was flat, but it was good to have its extra help. The coloured lights came into view and the drumming. Crowds covered the ground. Standing at the back, we were just able to make out the parade, some distance in front. There were various groups, each with much the same arrangement. I felt sorry for the elephants. The first had its cloth-covered ears surrounded in lights, with a pagoda arrangement of lights on its back. This must have been dreadful for the elephant, no longer being able to flap its ears to keep cool. Each elephant was followed by dancers and drummers in fantastic costumes. With all the glare of lights and noise of trumpets and drums, the poor elephants must have felt the human race had gone mad. We failed to see how any of this could have a religious connection. But then so must non-Christians look upon our celebrations at Christmas and feel the same. Colourful it most certainly was, and it was clear that everyone was in a happy mood. It was the elephants I watched the most. They had heavy colourful drapes over them while one or two were in their birthday suit, small ones, perhaps learning the trade. One elephant tried to get out of line but was enticed back. Why do we have to treat any animal so. A Buddhist once told me that it is a great honour for the elephant to be a temple elephant and take part in Holy Festivals. Perhaps those who believe that and believe in reincarnation will come back as a temple elephant. I found a box and sat down. Manny told me there was still much more to see, but I had seen enough and was only too thankful when it was decided to return to the Lodge.

Manny, who was not a well man at the time, said he had special painkillers – a bottle of arrack. To our surprise, it was only ten-thirty, and he invited us to join him in a drink before bed. We declined his offer and naughtily reminded him it was Poya when any consumption of alcohol is prohibited. After arranging to leave the next morning at five, we said our goodnights.

We were woken early by the manager of the Lodge knocking on our door. We were out and drinking our tea, but only Manny was up. This was amazing as he had stayed up until two that morning with the manager emptying the bottle of arrack. Our guide-to-be was also ready, but the rest of the family emerged one by one rather later. Six people all having to wait their turn to use the bathroom. The manager looked at my passport and confirmed that I should only pay the local price to get into Yala. Good news which would have been even better if Michael had not left his passport behind.

At last, we were going to see animals living naturally. It looked good for seeing a sloth bear after passing a jeep that had been watching one eating the Palu berries and pointed out the path. Some berries still remained, but the bear had had its fill and gone. Our last trip had been in December 2010 when it all looked so much greener. This time it was July four years later, now the wet areas were dry caked mud. The guide cheered us up by saying it would be easier to see animals as so many of the water holes had dried up. The authorities had made and filled more water holes, and the animals would go to those. True, except the sloth bears and leopards must have quenched their thirst earlier or elsewhere. We just managed to see some birds, but in a low vehicle, our view was limited. I, being in front with an open window, had the best position but only if what we were wishing to see was on my side. Michael was less fortunate, and the rest did not appear bothered at not seeing much.

Wild pigs entertained us for a while. We spotted a bull elephant trying to hide behind a leafless bush, later 2 females with their young. Mongooses were plentiful, and we spotted deer and water birds. Buffaloes and crocodiles were the easiest to see, with only one langur spotted. We had driven around for five and a half hours, Manny saying he would not give up until we saw a leopard. Sadly, we agreed this was not going to happen. It was good of Manny to arrange the trip, and hardly his fault we saw so little life. If we go again, we agreed it would be far better to go in one of the elevated vehicles.

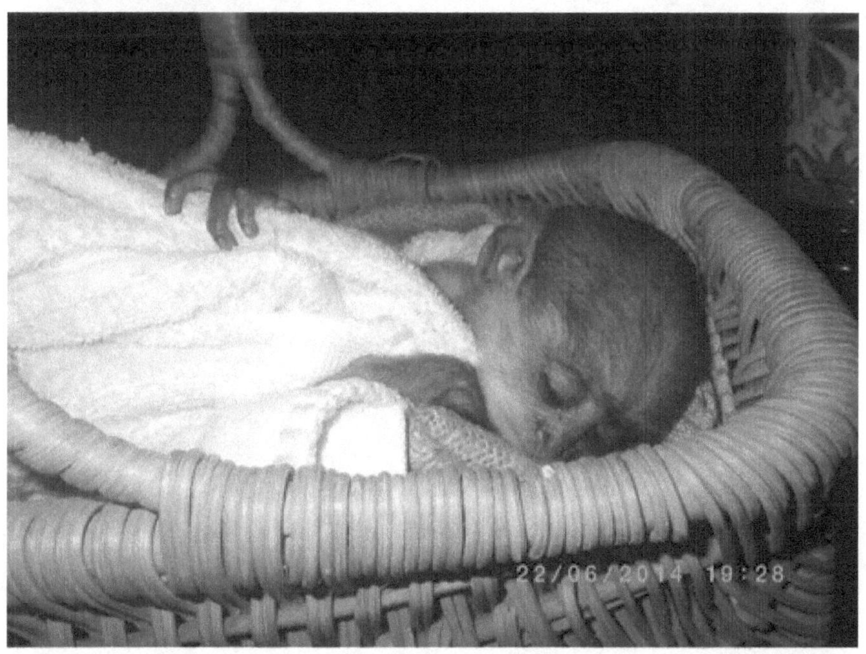

Tiny Tim

Miss Muffit

Lucy says hello ro Miss Muffit

Rattus bwfore his eyes opened

Chapter Twenty One

Monkey Business

While feeling I could not be happier in our chosen new home, there was one thing missing. The purple-faced leaf monkeys we had been told were always to be seen remained absent until about six months after our arrival. Just the occasional sighting of one dashing across the drive or flinging itself from tree to tree across the road. The first real connection with one was totally unexpected.

Early one Sunday morning, Michael and I were in the kitchen when Bandusena appeared trying to tell us something. All we understood was baby and two hundred rupees. After further tries at trying to make us understand, he went out and we heard him roaring off on his scooter. When he returned, he had a large cardboard box strapped to his scooter. He was smiling as we stood in expectation, waiting for him to untie the mysterious box. When the box was opened, I failed to understand what it was I was looking at; it looked like a piece of raw meat. He lifted it out gently, a tiny monkey, just a few weeks old, met my eye. How it still lived, I don't know; it had the most terrible wounds. At first, I thought it must have been attacked by dogs. While I have tended many an animal that needed love and care, I am no doctor or vet. I knew we needed a vet and fast. I said Tuk-tuk, and Bandusena phoned while I wrapped the poor little mite in towels. I moistened its lips with water, with no response. At that time, I had no idea where we might find a vet. Our driver was good and found a number of places with vet nameplates. At each, he took down the number and phoned, mostly with no response. It was Sunday; most would not open. Some only in the afternoon or at the best, ten in the morning. We finally found one that said he could arrive in half an hour's time. Then another that had been phoned returned his call. On hearing the problem, he said he would go straight away to his clinic. Back we went the way we had come through town. Dr. Senaka was there. The wounds were quite horrific; most of its back had all the flesh exposed. One kneecap also was just an open wound. The clinic was very small, mostly a glass room with a metal table on which the vet spread newspaper. I held the wee thing as the vet gave it an injection to put it to sleep. It did not take long before the injection worked. The vet cleaned the wound and found enough of the skin on its back to sew up. I could not look; I stood holding the monkey's head in my hands. The vet then said, "You know what I am doing might be all for nothing." I felt myself swaying and about to faint. Moving away, I sat on the step. I was given a chair and a glass of water. When the back had been stitched, the knee was examined, but there was no flap of skin. To draw the skins together would mean that the knee would not be able to bend. The whole operation appeared to take ages, and then he injected painkillers and antibiotics. If the monkey lived, we were to return in 48 hours or take it to an animal hospital that returns injured animals when well to the wild. Our driver said he knew the place and had the phone number.

Back home, I put towels in a shopping basket, which made a nice cradle and easy to move around. The Soya milk I mixed up, I administered with a tiny spoon and an eye dropper. He took it, but at once threw up. I phoned the hospital number the vet had given and talked to Madura de Silva. I was told to give it cow's milk. Could that be found on a Sunday morning near where we lived? We tend not to notice things for sale that we do not use. Michael went off in search, returning with a carton of liquid milk. That went down well and stayed down. I kept Tiny Tim, as I found myself calling him, with me the whole day. He preferred to be held by either me or Michael than put in the basket. He made little bird-like cries which puzzled the dogs. Bandusena did the cooking and kept Blackie and Rosie away. Pee Wee, the black and white young dog that had moved in, was surprisingly good, making no attempt to jump up and see what it was we were holding. I figured if it lasted the night, there was a chance of a recovery. It had the sweetest little face. The sad fact I now believed was that his appalling injury was likely inflicted by one of its own kind, a male taking over a troop and killing any youngsters. Not uncommon in the animal world, which includes humans. I slept with it that night. At first, he stayed in his basket next to me but later lay under my chin. By morning, he had moved between me and the basket, lying on his tummy. He had survived the night. I had taken some milk to bed with us and offered it to him, but he put out his little hand and gently pushed it away. Later, I warmed some milk from the fridge and he took it readily, then fell asleep. Laying him in the basket while we took breakfast, I covered his back with a light hankie to keep any flies off.

He remained sleeping, the hankie rising and falling as he breathed. Then the movement got slower and slower until finally we could not detect any movement. Lifting the cloth, I felt him move, but his little hand failed to clasp my finger. Michael and I tried breathing life into the little form and gently rubbing his heart, to no avail. Bandusena came and confirmed what we knew but did not wish to accept. Our tiny patient had passed away at about 10:30 that morning. We all felt its loss and decided to bury it behind the cashew tree where we sit of an evening. Bandusena dug a deep grave and lined it with leaves. We laid the little form wrapped in a tea towel with a leaf covering its face. Later, we planted a white Bougainvillea to mark the spot.

Our administrations had been a failure, but word must have got around as about four months later two men came up our drive with a sack. A sack containing yet another badly injured monkey. This time it was much older, about five months, with a better chance of living but with its left arm and both sides where the legs join the body dreadfully wounded. The first one had arrived on an early Sunday morning and this one on the evening of a Poya day, an even more difficult day to find anyone working. Bandusena had just arrived back from the temple when the men arrived. We phoned the vet and the wildlife centre, but neither replied. Our Tuk-tuk arrived and drove us straight to the vet who had operated on Tiny Tim. Michael came with me, which was fortunate since he had the forethought to carry a flashlight. It was dark when we arrived. No vet. People in the building next to the clinic room phoned; ten minutes later, the vet arrived. Miss Muffet, as Michael named her, was still quite strong, considering how bad her injuries were. She bit Michael, just a small nip but very sharp teeth.

Only one low-wattage bulb hung above the table the vet operated on. This time the vet had two female assistants; one held a small flashlight, Michael added his. When the vet thought he had done, Michael pointed out yet another unattended wound. Like me, the vet felt this one had a better chance of surviving. It was almost eight by the time Miss Muffet was repaired. As it was Poya, he said he could not charge. I gave him something; he said it was too much, handed some back.

At home, we received a nice welcome. Bandusena and Lucy, now very much my puppy, were waiting for us. Lucy was very good, though excited, upset I had gone away. The towel Miss Muffit had been wrapped in was covered in blood, and she remained out to the world. Bandusena got one of the packing boxes our goods had come in and added a clean towel. We cut windows in the box so she could, when waking, see out, then placed her in a spare bedroom. At bedtime, I felt it would not be a wise move to take her to bed with me as by then I shared my bed with Lucy. Instead, I put the box with her still sleeping in the connecting bathroom. I heard when she woke, she had got out of the box and was sitting in the shower, perhaps finding it cooler.

Our little miss appeared very alert but made no attempt to move around. She accepted milk and pineapple juice, disapproved of the leaves I provided but ate some of a green banana. Her right hand must have been useless as she never used it. The awful wounds at the top of her legs appear not to give her any trouble. Michael and I took it in turns to hold her when we showered, etc. I tried to phone Madura several times, but there was no reply. I discovered she preferred to sit next to me rather than being held in a towel. Her normal diet would be leaves. The predominantly leaf diet serves as an important energy source that their stomach is adapted to cope with. However, these monkeys in the west of the island now find they are living in areas taken over by humans, with fruit trees in most gardens they have adapted to a diet somewhat different from that found in the wild. They are still wary of humans and rarely come down to the ground but are quite happy to raid trees of unripe fruit. In our garden, they went mostly for jackfruit and bananas, also helping themselves to mangoes and soursop, taking a few bites and then tossing the rest on the ground in a spirit of generosity, thinking we might enjoy the fruit they can pick so much easier than us, or so I like to imagine. Miss Muffet spent a lot of time sleeping. At first, we thought it was good for her to get over what must have been a shocking experience. Two days later, she still showed no desire to move. Feeling it was time for her to get some exercise, we put a clothes rail in the courtyard and placed her on it. She at once urinated, a good start as we felt sure she had not done so until then. She also appeared much happier and ate leaves and banana, staying on the spot we had put her. We lifted her down to explore and realised she was far more crippled than we had thought. Only her left hand worked. Putting it on the ground, she moved along on her bottom making for the soursop tree. As if thankful to see a tree once more, she rested her left hand on the trunk. We lifted her up on a branch but lifted her back down before she fell. Lucy had stayed in the yard with her, and she showed no sign of being worried. Perhaps they would become friends. We discussed building a platform in the tree. Our hope of getting her well enough to return to the wild seemed no longer a possibility. Our task would be to make her life as happy as possible.

It was not to be. Next morning, we found she had died in the night. Perhaps she realised, as we had, that she would never obtain a life living in the trees. The photos of her show that her eyes looked bright and alert; the thought that she would not survive the night had not entered our heads.

There was now another little grave next to Tiny Tim's to plant a white bougainvillea on. Thankfully, no more injured monkeys came our way. As a nurse, I had failed miserably. In terms of saving lives, I was a complete failure.

We had been in the house for just two months when a baby rat fell down from the rafters just outside of the kitchen into the courtyard. He was uninjured, so I had high hopes of weaning him and returning him to the wild. Rattus's eyes were still closed, and he was quite unaware of what was happening to him. After taking a little soya milk, he nestled down in a plastic bowl of paper and grass. Rattus liked being held, and that evening we took him up to where we had the bench and hammock. I tried to put him on the ground; he was not keen, preferring my hand to exploring. Michael and I loved our little Rattus. Bandusena surprised us by showing he was not keen and wanted nothing to do with Rattus. On the third day, Rattus opened his eyes. If it was a surprise to him to see how large his parents were, he never showed it. He then drank from a spoon and liked nothing better than to have his tummy rubbed. When not about our person, he was happy to stay in his bowl. Knowing that one day he would wish to return to the wild, we continued taking him outside with us, though he still showed no interest in exploring.

Rattus had been part of our family for just eight days. While we were watching birds one evening, something startled him and he ran. This was the first time he had shown he could run. He made for the ground under the cashew tree. We searched and called, but he was lost in all the thick undergrowth. We left his bowl, food, and soya milk where we had last seen him, cursed our carelessness, and hoped he would be able to cope and survive. We never saw him again.

Feeding Rattus

Chapter Twenty Two

Strange Things Happen

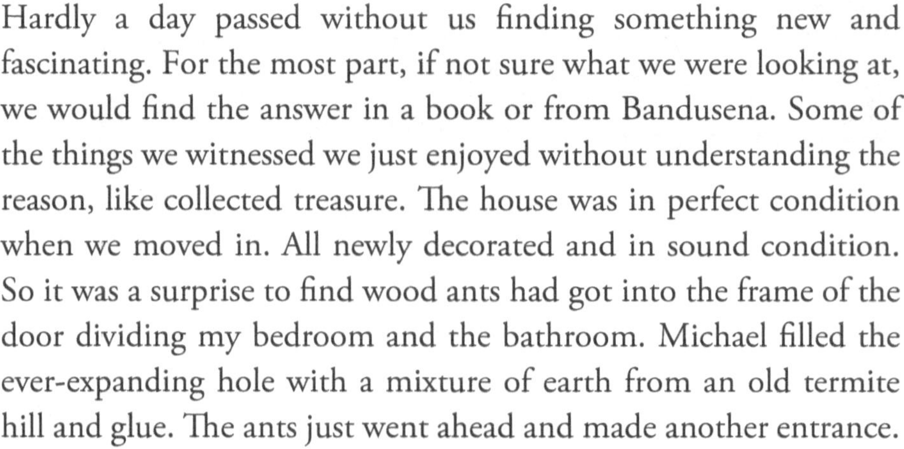

Hardly a day passed without us finding something new and fascinating. For the most part, if not sure what we were looking at, we would find the answer in a book or from Bandusena. Some of the things we witnessed we just enjoyed without understanding the reason, like collected treasure. The house was in perfect condition when we moved in. All newly decorated and in sound condition. So it was a surprise to find wood ants had got into the frame of the door dividing my bedroom and the bathroom. Michael filled the ever-expanding hole with a mixture of earth from an old termite hill and glue. The ants just went ahead and made another entrance.

One day, I found a beautiful iridescent green beetle, quite dead, being carried off by large black ants.

I stole it from them and brought it into my office, putting it under the microscope. I left it there so Michael and Bandusena could take a look. A short time later, seeing Michael, I told him and off he went to take a look, returning almost at once, saying he could not see it. The beetle was quite large and of such a brilliant colour, lying on the white plate under the microscope. I failed to understand how he could not see it. I went myself; I also failed to see it. "Perhaps the ants you took it from have taken it back," Michael suggested. Hardly possible, I had found it in the grounds a good hundred meters from the house.

There is a connecting door between the office and my bedroom. On the other side of the bedroom is the door to the bathroom. I found the missing beetle on the floor outside the wood ants' latest hole. Ants are not always welcome, and we put chalk around things we wish to protect from them. They are, however, one of the little marvels of life with such interesting lives. Many people have spent their lives studying certain species of ant.

These small black ants had crossed the bedroom, gone through the door of the office, climbed up to the desk and made their way to the beetle. All that to decorate their entrance. This we accepted, knowing how clever these wee creatures are, but had not before realised they appreciated pretty things. What followed some weeks later was far more astonishing.

Entering the bathroom one day, I noticed, around the door frame, a large number of sequins. Not being in the habit of sprinkling sequins about, it was obvious that the ants had a hand in this strange decoration. Where could they have found all these sequins was the puzzle. I had a skirt with sequins on, but that lay in a drawer. Surely they had not got in the drawer and hunted among all my clothes in search of something bright and shiny. Unlikely as it was, I took a look at the skirt finding it still intact. I sat on a stool looking at the ant hole surrounded by sequins in the hope of seeing the wood ants and discovering what their game was. The ants failed to appear. I stood up, then remembered the cushion I was sitting on was one of many bought in Morocco. The one on the stool had sequins sewn on in lines. I picked up the cushion and looked,

I found one remaining sequin. The threads attaching them to the cushion were still visible; each thread had been cut. I own three books on ants, none tell of this magpie-like tendency.

Blackie, as recorded earlier, had been spayed. This prevented her from having any more puppies of her own but, it transpired, did not stop her from producing milk and mothering two puppies that had turned up in the coop compound. Two very cute and very young female puppies must have been dumped there. Blackie and Rosie had made their home with us but still visited friends in the compound, both canine and human. When I saw Blackie lying down in the compound with the twins suckling her, I at first thought it must be another dog. Dogs that look like Blackie were quite common. It did turn out to be Blackie, and sometimes they followed her home, and I saw she actually was producing milk for them. When the puppies got a little older and started eating, being no longer in need of a wet nurse, Blackie, having fulfilled her duty, took no more interest in them. Blackie is a large and strong dog, not hesitating to bite a human or fight another dog if she feels it is justified. She also shows empathy with her own kind and with us, understanding if we are not feeling well or upset.

Rosie is much older and a clown. Small and extremely independent. Towards the end of our second year, we had hired a van and after much effort got all the dogs to enjoy outings. I had done some shopping and among other things had bought ten eggs. Michael stopped and popped into a supermarket and bought two slices of cake for my upcoming birthday. Shopping and cake were in the back of the van. The dogs move about while driving, between sitting up front, on the seats in the centre, or very occasionally in the back where there is a bowl of water for them.

Arriving home, about to carry the shopping in, we were greeted by the sight of an open cake box, devoid of a single crumb of cake. The box of ten eggs had also been lifted out of the bag, and all ten eggs neatly opened and eaten. She is a slow but dainty eater and there was no mess left behind. She showed no sign of guilt. Perhaps, she thought it had been put next to the bottle of water and the drinking bowl for her. What was surprising was that the other two dogs, like us had been blissfully unaware of the feast Rosie was enjoying. It was their dinner time when we got home, and Rosie joined the other two in the kitchen. Feeling sure she would not be able to To eat any more, I put down Lucy's and Blackie's dinner and just a few bits of dried dog food on Rosie's plate. She ate them and gave me a look as if to say, 'come on, where is the rest?' She still had room for her dinner.

Lucy is the baby of the family. From just a cute puppy, she grew into the most loving companion anyone could hope to have. Unlike her mother, Blackie, or Rosie, she has never had a hard life, gone hungry, or been ill-treated, yet she remains nervous of people she does not know. On the other hand, she loves and trusts her few friends. I am unable to go even just down the road to a local shop without her getting in a panic and crying. The other two may follow me and sit outside the shop, but Lucy is afraid, for some reason, to go out of the gate. She loves playing, something local people are surprised about. The idea of playing games with a dog is not something they had thought of. Having chased and caught a ball from a baby, she can catch anything tossed to her, unlike the other two. She also had a playmate when very young. Crows are common, but in our garden, we never saw any until one day a single crow arrived wanting to play with Lucy. The crow would sit on the roof.

Until Lucy saw it and then flew down with Lucy in hot pursuit. They would go round and round in a circle until the crow flew back on the roof and then down to play again. That crow, as it turned out, was not unusual. To this day, when we go to the beach with the dogs where there are crows, the dogs will go flat out trying to catch them, and the same crows will come back for more, teasing them.

In two and a half acres, the number of insects and other small creatures is limitless. The first time I saw what I think is called a horned spider, I was not sure I was looking at a spider. I like spiders, but beautiful is not a word I would choose to describe them. These almost triangular spiders are like little jewels. Their bodies are tastefully painted, and their legs are small and discreetly tucked under their bodies, barely visible. I soon found more when I had unwittingly walked into their orb web that would stretch low and at some length between bushes or trees. As far as I could tell, they change their site every day. If I found one in the morning and visited it several times, but the next morning it was gone.

To see a flutter of butterflies is a heartwarming experience, but for most of us, not a common one. Sitting on the patio one afternoon, we caught sight of a few white flecks in the sky, above and below the treetops. At first, we thought that someone had burnt paper and it was ash flecks. Then more arrived, white or pale yellow; we were not quite sure. They all flew in one direction, raggedly, and continued to pass all afternoon, and still more came the following day. We were unable to find out just what kind of butterflies they were and where they were heading. It made us happy just seeing them.

On the slight hill above the house where we enjoyed bird watching, there were a large number of trees apart from coconut palms. People always warned us about snakes, but we never saw any in that part of the plantation. Coconut palms are beautiful and the most all-round useful plants ever; however, they also very often kill people when they drop one of their heavy nuts on a person below. We were always very careful where we hung our hammock. In that area, we had a group of tall slender trees. We never found out what they were as when we asked, we were told they had no use and we might as well get rid of them. A tree should not have to be useful to be loved, and we were fond of them and called them the sisters. As with all things in nature, they had a part to play. Seeing something strange on the trunk of one of these trees, I took a closer look. What at first sight looked like a mat or piece of cloth stuck to the tree turned out to be an amazing number of caterpillars, nose to tail, leaving no space between. We observed them over a number of days and found smaller colonies on some of the other 'sisters'.

The large mass moved first. Slowly, one caterpillar on the outer edge would detach itself from the mass and start up the trunk. The rest would follow in a rather badly organised line, mostly single file, but often some would break ranks and make it double. The leader did not hold his position for long, every now and then, he would be overtaken and another would take the lead. The tree was very tall, and I expected they were headed for the leaves. It is not often that you need binoculars to see caterpillars. Soon, my binoculars were the only way I could still see them. They reached the leaves, not stopping for a snack, but continued upwards. That was the last I saw of them as they got out of sight, obscured by branches. That they would turn into moths, I was sure, but I would have liked to have found out what kind. I sent an email to a society in Colombo that I thought would enlighten me. Sometime later, I received a reply. They confirmed it was one of two kinds of moth. What kind they did not say.

Not all of our unexpected sightings were found outside. One evening we were besieged by unexpected but very welcome visitors. We were sitting reading when, plop! A tree frog landed on my book. He was a very handsome chap. Finding my book less interesting than I had, he jumped off. Where he went, neither of us could see. In looking for him, Michael discovered two male toads. I finally spotted my frog on the back of the chair I had been sitting on. He made another leap and landed on the wall, his suction-padded feet allowing him to make his way right up to the high ceiling. Having enjoyed that evening's entertainment, I took myself off to bed. Before falling asleep, Michael came in and said, "I think there is an owl in the living area."

"An owl," I repeated in disbelief. "Do you mean a bat?" "No, an owl," he stressed. I got up, not really expecting to see an owl. At first, I saw nothing. Then there it was, a little owl sitting on the head of a carving from Fiji on top of a tall bookshelf. It gave a long wink. We would have been happy for it to stay the night, but after resting and having its photo taken and not being offered anything in the way of food, it flew back out to the courtyard. It then flew down to the ground. At first, we thought it might be injured or a baby, but it looked OK and flew off.

Another visitor that would join us each night as the sun went down was a magpie robin. In the centre of the ceiling was a modern hanging lamp. It was not our choice, and we never turned it on. Like a lot of things, it did turn out to have its uses. It had a metal ring around it on which the robin

would perch and settle down for the night. Magpie robins are friendly birds, and we would feed this one on a big rock outside the kitchen so that we felt honoured rather than surprised.

Early one morning, Michael was woken by noise and movement in his room. Turning the light on, he saw a cat jump out of the window. This was strange as we did not have a cat and knew of none. Wherever it had come from, it must have walked some distance to get to the house. Michael's door leading into the living area was open, where Blackie and Rosie were sleeping; they had made no attempt to see what the fuss was about.

Hearing the commotion, I got up and noticed the magpie robin was not on the lamp. When Michael saw that, he said he had got the impression that the cat was after a bird. Getting down on our hands and knees, we looked under Michael's bed. There was the magpie robin; it was not damaged as far as we could see, so we left it with a bowl of water and food, closing the bedroom door to keep the dogs out. Later, it had gone. Not surprisingly, we never saw it again.

Why did we ponder if the bird had flown down to be caught by a cat that we had never seen before or after? The dogs like to chase anything that runs but had let all that take place without moving or barking. The whole episode left us with a big question that we would never be able to answer.

Magpie Robin slept on the rings round our central light

Night visitors small owl sat on a Fiji carving.

Tree frog climbed our wall

Emerald beetle

Orb spider we call TT

Another orb spider

Chapter Twenty Three

Sinhala-Tamil New Year

In Galle, the atmosphere, not the weather, was a little like Christmas in the UK. The traffic was, if possible, even worse than usual, and the street packed with shoppers. Stalls had sprung up where no stalls were before. Preparations were being made for the Sinhala/Tamil New Year that would take place on April 14th. The name New Year is a little different. Their calendar year starts on January the first. We were told it was like a thanksgiving for a good harvest.

We joined the crowd to buy a shirt, sarong, and some new clay cooking pots. These, with money, would be a New Year gift to Bandusena. Our friends had made sure we knew the rules, and we were rather keen to partake in whatever celebrations might be going on.

We were not quite so keen when the day before New Year Bandusena indicated that both Michael and I should go with him to the traditional kitchen. He had two bags of stuff to show us. One we recognised as dry clay from a termite hill. The other, still closed, smelt strongly of rotten vegetables. Was this the makings for our lunch? We looked at each other in dismay. Bandusena had turned out to be a wonderful cook, often preparing a dish from what looked like to us, weeds from the garden or odd-looking vegetables, but all had tasted delicious. We then noticed the big fireplace had been cleaned, leaving just the stands on the cooking counter for the cooking pots. With goggled eyes, we watched as he emptied the bag of dry clay, broke it into bits, added water, and began kneading it like dough. He then opened the other bag. It was not rotten vegetables. What he emptied out was a pile of wet cow or buffalo dung. We stood speechless.

The second ingredient was added to the first and again kneaded until mixed to one consistency. We were, of course, fully aware by now that he was not preparing anything to eat. Still, why was he doing this in the kitchen and on the area he had just cleaned? We understood when he started to spread, by hand, this strange mixture all over the cooking counter, which before had been looking a bit cracked. The end result was a brand-new surface, ready now for the new cooking pots.

Mixing termite clay and cow or buffalo dung

New cooking surface

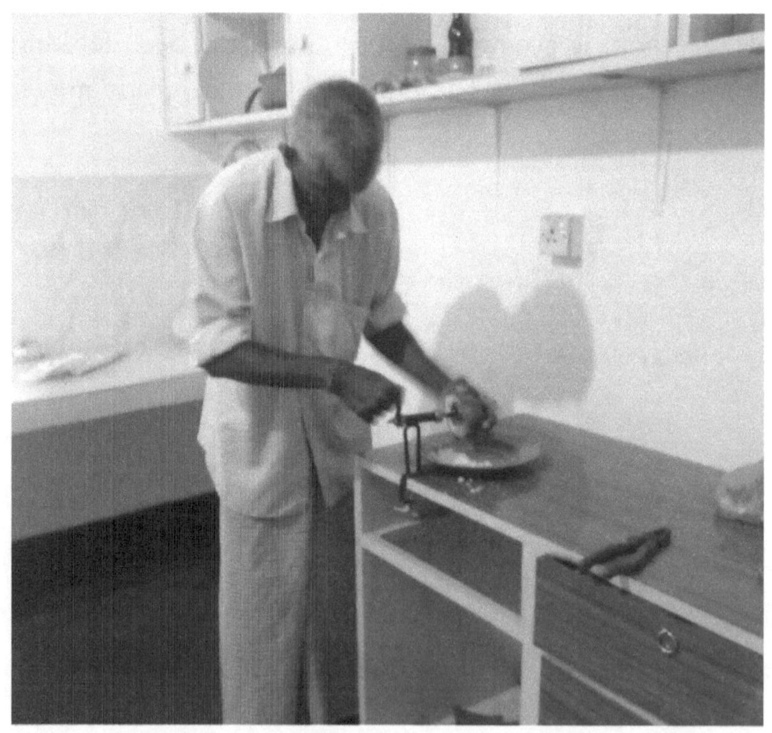

grating coconut

Cooking red rice.

A harth and fire in the living area to boil coconut milk to purify the house

Pounding leaves

Using the grinding stone

We woke the following morning, New Year, to see some of our chairs in the living area had been pushed back leaving a larger area in the centre of the room. This area now had a square piece of wood, placed on bricks on the floor, topped with a sheet of metal with three further bricks in the centre. This was something that might find itself in the Tate in London but not the type of art we liked. We found Bandusena was busy outside grating a large amount of coconut. Later, one of the small cooking pots we had purchased was filled with the freshly made coconut milk, then balanced on the three bricks. Bundles of dry grass and coconut husks were laid nearby.

After watching the building of this new addition to our living area, we followed him into the kitchen again. It was a very still morning, with very little traffic, just the odd scooter, a few pops, and bangs as someone let off firecrackers. Michael and I now watched as Bandusena mixed tomatoes, onions, and chillies and make a tasty sambal dish, of which I was invited to taste.

Back we went into the living area. At 10:15, more pops and bangs indicated it was time for the next move. Bandusena handed me a bunch of dry grass, lighting it so I could light the fire under the pot of coconut milk. More fuel was added. Leaving the fire unattended, we trooped back into the kitchen. Rice was washed, salt added, and coconut milk all put in one of the new cooking pots. Fire was lit under the pot. Back again into the house to see how the pot of coconut milk was getting on. Perfect timing, as we watched the coconut milk come to a boil and overflow. Our house was now cleansed.

Back again in the kitchen. Bandusena having removed the remains of the fire under the coconut milk. The bricks, etc., he carried out and left to cool in the courtyard. The milk rice had, in the meantime, cooked and was turned out onto a plate. This was smoothed out into a perfect mound, using a banana leaf. Leaving the rice and sambal on the counter, we were told to eat it at eleven o'clock. Rather early for us. We disobeyed, leaving it for later. There is, during this celebration, a time for everything. At the time, we were blissfully unaware of it. Bandusena had gone to his home and family who had to celebrate without him. We did not expect him back that day but were surprised when he soon returned, bowing low. He handed each of us a betel leaf. I still have mine in the pages of my most useful book on tropical gardening.

Tropical Planting and Gardening with special reference to Ceylon - H.F. Macmillan LJS phoned to say he and his family would be coming to visit us. In fact, it was the next day they showed up. Manny and his family paid us a visit, giving us more milk rice, sambal, and the same cookies Bandusena had made by dipping a shaped metal tool in batter and then in hot oil. We were not going to be short of things to eat. Manny also had a bag of books for us. I had mentioned the thing I was most keen to see again when our shipment arrived would be our books. Manny said he had some very old books I could read. I said I would love to read them, visualising antique books about Ceylon. I hope I hid my disappointment when I saw what the bag contained: paperback novels with yellowing pages. Later, we were able to give them back, saying the print was too small to read, which in fact it would have been had we tried to read them.

Bandusena returned again, wearing the shirt and sarong we had given him. We asked Manny to tell him he did not have to stay and could spend the rest of the day with his family. His reply was that the noise of the children in his house was too much, and he preferred to go to his room to rest.

Two days later, we went in search of open shops. Most were still closed as a continuation of the holiday. Since all the little grocery shops were privately owned, they opened and closed at the whim of the owners. It was a nice, relaxed attitude unless you were desperate for a particular food item.

Returning home with little to show for our hunt, we found LJS and his family awaiting us. LJS was in his charming mood, and we were able to enjoy their visit. They too had brought us a gift of a five-kilo bag of rice, along with more homemade cookies. We had nothing to offer except the cookies and cold water.

LJS did have a strange proposal. He was in touch with an English lady who needed to be in Galle for a period of ten weeks. He suggested she stay with us. He then got her on the phone and handed it to me to talk to her. I explained we were still awaiting our shipment but would be happy to meet her one day if she so wished. We certainly would not want a stranger staying for ten weeks, and I doubted that she was a vegetarian. We heard no more on the subject.

The New Year celebrations were the first we took part in, soon after our arrival. There was More holidays to come with 25 public holidays a year. People coming here to do business find this rather a handicap, even more so when they return to Europe and are not sure when the holidays fall and the time difference. We felt it was the right attitude. Each religion had its holidays. All banks and government departments had all the holidays off. Private businesses were free to decide whether to close or not.

Poya days were days when the moon was full. Each month, the Poya day celebrates an incident in the life of the Buddha. The most important of these is Vesak Poya, remembering the anniversary of the Buddha's birth, enlightenment, and passing. It also had an added attraction here in Sri Lanka; the local belief being; when the Buddha paid his third and last visit to the island.

Vesak Poya was very colourful. Living in an area predominantly Buddhist, we were able to enjoy it to the full. Lanterns were hung outside nearly all houses and businesses, ranging from all white to multi-coloured ones with very long streamers. Unfortunately, they are very often shrouded in long plastic bags to protect them from the weather and dirt that spoil the overall effect. Masses of white ones, all in plastic, hanging along roads look like nothing more than plastic bags, and one visitor thought it was something to do with banning plastic. Rather the reverse.

Complete lanterns can be bought. Many still prefer to make their own. Tissue paper in various colours is available, and for the less nimble, plastic frames can also be purchased that are easy to assemble. I had read in an article that originally everyone made their own lanterns, making the frames from split bamboo. By showing a picture of a lantern and a bit of sign language, I asked Bandusena if he could make a lantern. He said, "Yes". However, I was not sure he understood the whole question.

Next day, I noticed some long bamboo canes outside his room. Later, I found him cutting thin strips off the cane, then making sure they were all of the same length. He started making the frame. With the canes already cut, the rest looked easy. I sat on the ground next to him and joined two together. It was the third cane that was the hard part; with me, it resulted in the first joint falling apart. For someone who prides themselves on being good at handicrafts and being able to see how things can be done, this was a big comedown for me. Once again, I had to remind myself I was old and many things that were once easy were now becoming difficult or impossible. Ashamed, I gave up. Bandusena finished a frame, and I found some tissue paper to stick on the frame and used gold braid for trim. We now had our own Vesak lantern.

Lanterns were only a small part of the attractions. There were also huge pandols in all major towns. A pandol consists of a very tall scaffold frame. Traditionally, I am told, made from talipot palms or bamboo, but sometimes, these days, they use regular metal scaffold for the frames. The frames are then covered with coloured lights and pictures depicting the life of the Buddha. The actual design varies. I would like to know if anything similar was made before the discovery of electric light. I also wondered what Buddha would have thought of it all.

Bandusena returning from the temple with Rosie

By the sides of the roads, dansalas were set up. A dansala is a stall or even just a table with drinks and food or ice cream set up by groups of devotees. As cars pass, they are waved down and handed food or a drink quite freely. This, I felt, was more like the true spirit of the day, one that Buddha surely would have approved of. Inland, away from large roads, some really large dansalas were set up in tents, with benches to sit on and plates covered in plastic sheets, which the group setting it up ladle rice and various curries. In our second year, a dansala was set up on the edge of our rented property, and we got personal invites to attend. Lucy hung back, but Blackie and Rosie took up the invitation, which was a little embarrassing as we did not think dogs were invited. We sat near the entrance and prevented the dogs from going inside the tent.

Other Poya days are less flamboyant but to unaccustomed ears still very noisy. We often wished that the loudspeaker had never been invented. The Moslem call to prayer in the far past, in other countries I did not mind and in fact liked. In those days, it was the natural human voice that called. Now it's electronic. I have actually heard Buddhists complain. Perhaps retaliating with their own loudspeakers from which chanting, talking, and drums issue for long periods at high volume. After a very heavy rainfall one day, the rain must have got into the speakers at the temple. While we had never been able to understand anything, we doubted very much if anyone could distinguish what was being said. It sounded like underwater gurgling.

Bandusena cuts equal length bamboo strips

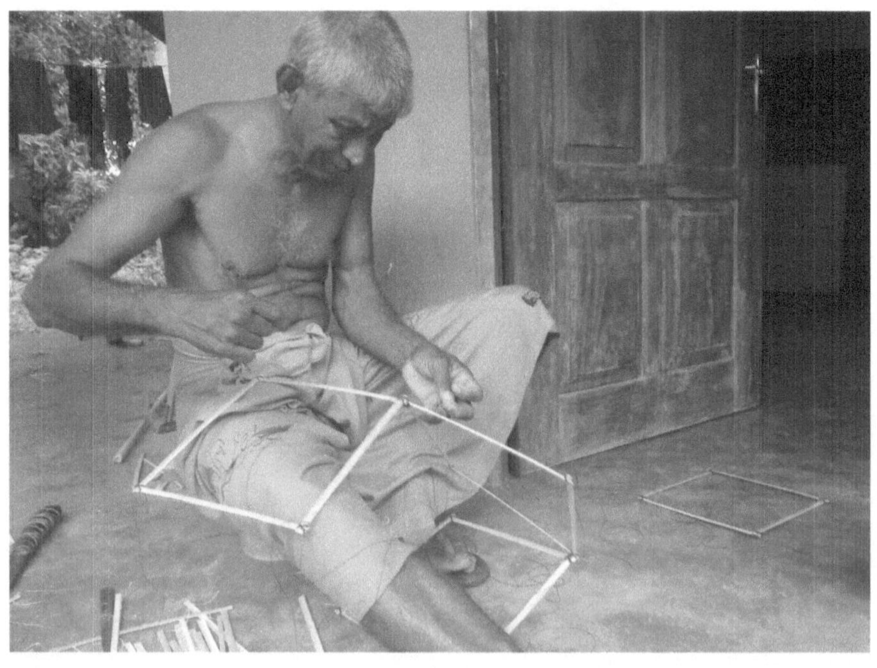

Joining the strips to make the frame

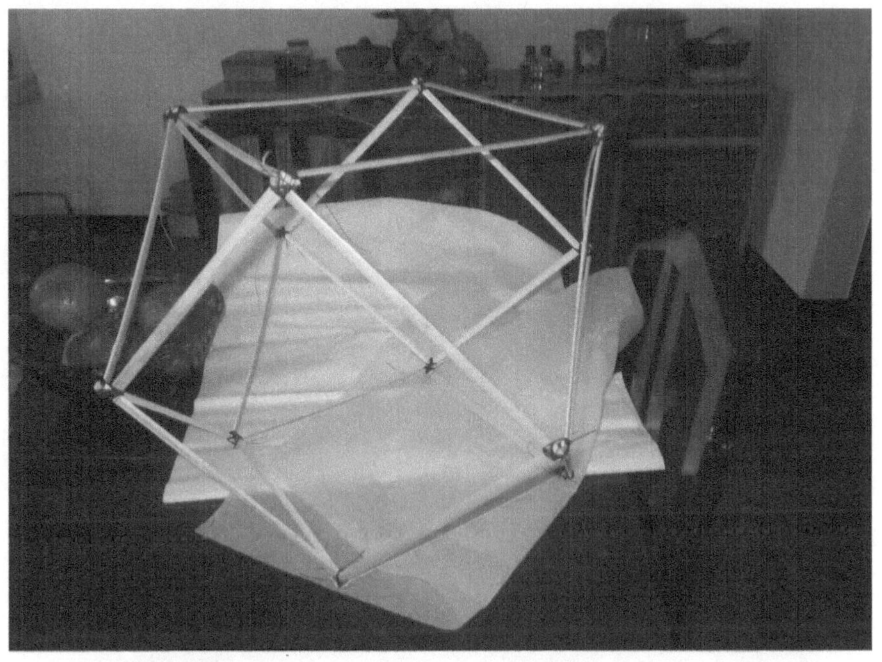

Frame before covering in tissue paper.

Lantern in place

Dansal outside our house grounds

On poya, people dress all in white and visit the temple. No beer, arrack, or any kind of alcohol is sold, and the majority of Buddhists keep to the rules.

Buddhism is very much a part of the Sinhalese way of life. It is probably partly due to having the monthly Poya day that helps keep traditions alive.

Apart from public celebrations, there were also private ones. We have yet to be invited to a wedding. We know it is the practice to hand out small pieces of wedding cake, proper fruit cake with icing, in small card boxes decorated with rings and bells, with the name and date of the wedding on the side. I had a small collection of these little boxes from which we had enjoyed the cake. For a while, I kept them, feeling they were too good to throw away. Bandusena appeared to regularly be invited to weddings, and on his return, he would give us a little box each. Once he went to three weddings in the course of four days. June, as in the UK, appears to be the popular month.

We also heard that people were going to an almsgiving. This sounded rather old fashioned to us, but we took it they were supporting a charity of some kind.

Our first experience of almsgiving was when Sita invited us to her almsgiving to celebrate her late husband's birthday. Not being quite sure what to expect, we asked Manny. "Take a tub of ice cream," he suggested, then added the most popular make. Having been told to arrive at noon, we told Garmeni, our tuk-tuk driver, to take us in time for our arrival at noon, also that we would have to stop off and buy ice cream on the way. It turned out he had not understood that we needed to arrive at noon. As time passed, we phoned. "I'm coming noon." "No, now," we replied. Time means little here as a rule, but he had understood rightly that this time we should be on time. Garmeni knew of a number of places that sold ice cream. It was not until the fourth stop that we were able to get the required kind. He still promised to get us there on time, and he would have had we not been held up in a traffic jam owing to a motorcycle accident. Then at the fort, we found two roads cordoned off, delaying us further. We arrived at Beach Haven to find the room very changed and full. Half the chairs were covered in white cloth upon which sat ten orange-robed monks with their traditional large fans. One was reciting something. We slid in, handing over the ice cream to Lalith who had seen us and got up. I hoped we were not being an embarrassment arriving so late; room was made for us to sit on the floor near Sita, joining the rest of the family and invited guests. There was plenty of time to observe the monks as when one finished reciting or praying, another had their turn. All looked very well-fed.

In front of them were low tables on which a green plastic bag was placed in front of each monk. Their takeaway goodie bag, we presumed. In the corner of the room was a stand on which I first took to be an urn. When all the reciting and prayers were finished, the monks rose and filed out.

No chit-chat or smiles. At this point, Sita's grandson got up and placed a cloth over his head. Picking up the urn, also covered, he carried it out on his head. His father, Lalith, stood outside with a large yellow silk umbrella. Outside was a car and one of the monks sitting next to the driver. The monk took the covered urn and snatched the cloth off the boy's head. I watched and was not convinced the monk was one of the ten that had been in the room. This one had a strange look on his face as if frightened. At that point, I thought the urn, if that is the correct word, held the ashes of Sita's late husband. Later, I learned it contained a replica of the Buddha.

The monks gone, we all trooped to the pantry to eat. Here was a wonderful array of dishes, perhaps a dozen or more. Even passing on the fish and chicken, our plates were overflowing. Shiromi had been busy and was a skilled cook. We felt very privileged to be part of this loving and close family.

When the first of January came round, it was yet another holiday. The evening before Bandusena told us we would eat rice for breakfast. We had no idea why and thought no more about it. Around five in the morning, Michael heard Bandusena pounding away in the kitchen. An hour later, we got up to find our breakfast waiting, a rounded milk rice covered with a banana leaf and chili sambal.

We had not anticipated that our New Year would also be celebrated in the local custom. Manny phoned: "Are you giving Bandusean a gift today?" A bit taken aback, I said "no, should I?" "Everyone has new clothes for the New Year. Give him a shirt or sarong." What I wondered, would we do without Manny advising us on the customs lest we inadvertently offend. I dashed down the drive to a nearby shop, mainly a tailor but had seen some ready-made shirts in the window. Picking a purple striped one, I asked if it would fit Bandusena; they said yes and if he did not like it, he could change it. I got back just in time to give it to him before he left for his house.

Chapter Twenty Four

One with the Land

From the day we moved in, we became obsessed with the land. Part of the charm was that it was so neglected and overgrown. I had a compelling urge to strip all the bushes of the vines that hid them from view, while making paths and putting a little order into some of the areas, still leaving the huge trees and much of the undergrowth to go its own way.

It was mainly a coconut plantation. The older coconuts had grown to great heights while the nuts that they dropped had taken root and were still growing. Owing to LJS, we had missed out on organising our first coconut picking, or plucking as they say here. Two months later, we did it ourselves. In truth, we did little, leaving the hiring of the picker and counting all the nuts as they were picked to Bandusena. With paper and pencil, he kept a tally of every palm picked and the number of nuts from each. On average, the coconuts were picked every second month from about 76 palms. The number of nuts from a single palm varied from five to twenty-five. This is not thought to be a good crop. The trees were old. We were urged to apply fertiliser but resisted and just piled cut grass and weeds around the roots. The picker/plucker was tiny and no youngster either. He would swarm up the tallest palm with ease. He had the same build as Michael, both lacking any extra flesh, the difference being he must have been about 18 inches shorter. Two young men came with him and collected the nuts as they were tossed to the ground and carried them to the large barn, forming a large pile. The picker was paid per palm, so collected quite a good wage at the end of the morning. A wage we were told would be spent on arrack. The collectors had the daily rate. Before they started work, they had to have tea. Bandusena saw to that, knowing they liked it strong and more to the consistency of syrup. Sugar with tea, I would have called it. Bandusena then would join them sitting outside his room for their tea and biscuits. The latter must have been in lieu of a meal. We had opened a packet of biscuits and put a number out for them and were about to put the rest away. Bandusena must have thought we were getting muddled and took the larger portion, that must have consisted of several biscuits per person. Finding buyers proved easy the first time as we had some friends promising to buy. Other times we were not so fortunate. Our dear friends from Beach Haven were the only ones to be relied upon to turn up on the expected day and time. When all the nuts were picked, we phoned people who had shown an interest. Naively, we noted down the time and day they would come and how many nuts they wanted. Apart from the aforementioned friends, no one turned up on the given day, let alone on time. We then changed to selling to anyone who arrived, upsetting others who came days later than promised to find all sold or not the amount they wanted left. We set the price, but this did not stop haggling and pronouncing that the nuts were small.

Our first priority was to get the money we had spent on having them picked. After that, Bandusena got a set amount, the rest was ours. Sometimes, it's touch and go whether we will make anything.

Mostly, buyers came in trucks, picking up each coconut and shaking it before tossing it in the truck, while we stand by counting how many they take. Some nuts are rejected but will be taken by the next buyer. After the novelty had worn off, it was hardly worth the bother for the profit we received. We continued as by having them picked there was a better chance of not being killed by a falling nut. Bandusena gained a little extra cash and of course, we kept enough for our own use.

Climbing a palm

At the top

Hundreds of coconuts to sell.

The tiny coconut picker with Michael who is six feet.

As we cleared paths to walk along, we discovered plants we had not been able to see before. At first, we went round the back of the house, climbing so we looked down on the roof. We cleared where we had the seat and had a big bonfire a short distance in front. This turned into a pile of ash, which Rosie felt made an even better place to lie than in pools of oil. Going back in the bush a little, we found the most marvelous tree. I called it the sacred tree and made a short path to its base. We never discovered what the tree was or even what it looked like. It was so festooned in other plant life, even small saplings. Before reaching its base, there was another tree that attracted our attention with its strange fruits. The yellow-coloured skin divided into sections, like a peeled orange with a small red bit inside that tasted very sweet. The fruit that had fallen on the ground mostly had the little sweet red treat taken by some foraging animal. It was a Goraka *Garcinia cambogia*, native to Sri Lanka. Bandusena would collect the fruit and set it out in the sun to dry after cutting apart the sections. The blackened sections were then used to preserve fish.

As we cleared the paths, we also hauled hundreds, if not thousands, of dead palm fronds that had fallen over the years. We had bonfires most days in two places, widely apart, we thought. As the clearing progressed, we could see more, and one day standing by one of the bonfire sites, we looked down and saw only about 50 meters away and lower down, our other fire. We soon had a trail that made a round trip from the front of the house to the back.

Fronds were not the only things we burned. The many vines that took over paths and other vegetation we soon found had no intention of being made into compost. Instead, they thrived unless burnt. When the Rambutan and Donker trees fruited and their seeds dropped, we soon had our paths covered in millions of wee tree seedlings.

The reward for all our work was finding plants spring up that were far superior to the vegetation that had once prevented them from appearing. Most were lily types with bulbs that had stayed below ground until the covered vegetation had been removed and they sensed the light above. The first delight was "Pixie palettes", our name for Caladium bicolour. They appeared in a variety of designs. By carefully clearing everything around the plants, we soon had a colourful display of these painted leaves. Finding another kind of lily leaf, we nurtured it. It rewarded us with a bright global flower, Blood Lily *Haemanthus puniceus*, several clumps of spider lily *Pancratium arenicolum*. We started finding some very strange plants that I had never seen before.

Varied in size, with spotted stems much like the stem of the blood lily but entirely different. Leaves unfolding from the top of the stem. They also grew from a tuber. If it was going to flower, it would have to be from the ground. I then thought I had found it pictured in H.F. Macmillan's wonderful book or thought I had. None of ours were as tall, but otherwise matched the picture. We would have to wait for the floral spathe.

The expected spathe never came that year, and some of those strange plants withered and died.

While shopping in the market one day, I spotted a tuber which looked remarkably like the one we had dug up. The local name was 'Kidaran'. When I suggested to Bandusean that the root could be eaten, he said, "No". The following year, a very strange flower materialised from the ground. A flower I never dreamed of finding. The gardening book gave no picture, only a description. *Amorphophallus campanulatus.* This had to be it. It was supposed to be strongly foetid. We nicknamed it the stinker, but we smelt nothing. We soon started finding several more stinkers, and then one day I smelt something bad and found another of the flowers living up to its name. It appeared they only smelt for one day, in which time they attracted flies and other insects. I sent photos to the Elizabeth Miller library with a description and received confirmation. It was the flower of the parent leaf but appeared after that died. They only flower every three or four years, so it was fortunate we found them. We found a number that year, so they were quite common. That did not diminish the pleasure we found in discovering them.

Plants that we had lovingly planted in our glass room in England like mother-in-law tongue and Monstera – Swiss cheese plant, we were now calling weeds and pulling them up. The Monstera was trying to cover all the trees, and while I still liked the leaves, it was only left on trees that had already died.

We had a number of plants of the ginger family which were interesting, plus of course the ginger root of which we used daily. Outside the kitchen, we had a whole bed of what I took to be heliconia. Then it flowered. I had no idea what it was. I pointed it out to Bandusena, and he went into the kitchen to show me the turmeric we use daily. I never guessed we were also growing it just outside.

We dug it up and soon had a pile of the roots laid out to dry. They soon looked dry enough to me to grind into powder, but no, they still had to shrivel up to nothing. The pounding of them was laborious and hardly worth it, I felt, when the powder was so readily available and cheap in the market. When our friend Manny visited and saw, he took them and got his wife to put them in the electric grinder. We also had cinnamon trees which Bandusena would cut off a branch and strip the outer bark as we had seen a peeler do some years before. That was a much easier task than preparing the turmeric. I only found out we had a clove tree when I inquired of Bandusean what a tall slender tree was that grew by the grave of the man who had built the house. I thought it might have some significant meaning. Another trip to the kitchen answered my query. The buds of the clove flowers could have been dried for use, had we been able to reach them.

Gloriosa, I was happy to find had popped up where it felt right; I was quite happy for it to clamber over taller plants or trees. It died after flowering but was a gentle plant.

Flanking the drive, we had pines! Four on each side and of various types. Had we been in Europe, they would have been acceptable. In the tropics, they were very out of place and gave too much shade, cutting out the tropical aspect of the place. They shed needles in bucket loads and prevented growth. Not even the vines had dared to attack them. They had grown to a domineering height, spoiling, I felt, the whole place.

We had a lovely landlady who let us do as we wished, but she liked the pines as her late husband, whose ashes lay in the garden grave, had loved and planted them. She agreed we could have five of them cut down and arranged for the men to come and remove them without harming other plants. The men were only too pleased to be getting so much wood, and the cutting down and removing was free. I was assured they would not let the trunks land on the beds they were in.

The men arrived. First, they sat on the grass and cleaned or fiddled around with a chainsaw while they chewed betel. One man climbed one of the pines until he reached the branches. With a large knife, he cut them off, tossing them down on the drive. Nearing the top, he secured a rope, then came halfway down. Lowering another rope, the chainsaw was secured to it, and he hauled it up. Making himself comfy in his lofty perch, he set about sawing the trunk above him. To us, this looked highly dangerous. By now, a number of men were stretched out along the drive, pulling at the rope tied to the top of the tree. As the cut was nearly finished, a shout was given, and everyone pulled, landing the trunk in a perfect position along the drive. Much as I wanted the removal of the pines, I did feel a pang of regret at the murder of this giant of a tree. The fallen part was then cut into lengths that would fit into the truck. The lower half was tackled in much the same way. The men were understandably getting tired as the third tree took out a lot of bushes before landing on the drive, where it had to stay the night as there was no more room on the loaded truck. The next day they were not so clever either, as the remaining one to be felled came down and took out one that was supposed to have remained. I was not too sorry and did wonder if it was by accident or design.

Halfway through, when the truck was loaded and should have left, the men downed tools and sprawled out on the grass. Bandusena had a word with one of the men. One of the men, with some English, told me they had seen a police car. I discovered later that to cut down a tree, they should have had a license.

One of the shrubs near the house remained bare of flowers. Then, suddenly, it burst into deep blue flowers, which the next day were light blue, and then white. The local name was "Yesterday, today and tomorrow."

It was always a treat to be able to look out of my bedroom window and see the large frangipani covered in its sweet-smelling white flowers. There was an added attraction first thing in the morning. A kingfisher would appear, and then another. They looked identical, but then one would start feeding the other. What a perfect start to the day.

The cactus from Italy had started growing a new section from the day it was released from its packing. Our landlady was amused when told we had brought it with us in our luggage along with a number of smaller ones. The big Italian one did survive, just. Bandusena not used to cacti had been watering it to death. The small ones vanished. I transferred the big one to a pot and, denying it water, it sprung to life, to Bandusena's surprise.

Weeding the very steep banks was not easy. I was starting from the top of one of the banks one day when I dropped the knife I was using. I was sure it had just dropped at my feet. Searching for ages where I felt it should be, I then started working my way down the slope, arriving at the bottom far faster than intended, I fell backwards. My fall was stopped when the leg of my pants caught on a stump, ripping the cloth and rendering me quite indecent. It took a lot of energy to claw my way back up. I must have looked quite interesting had there been anyone around to see me in ripped pants, covered in red mud, and bits of vegetation.

Much later, when we had cleared that bank and planted shrubs, we still had not found the knife. Well over a year later, Michael picked it up not too far from where I had dropped it.

Gardening did have its dangers. Everyone in Europe talked of mosquitoes in the tropics, as if they did not occur in other parts of the world. Yes, we had mosquitoes, but it was a certain few members of the ant family that were best avoided. Big red ants made their nest in trees by sewing leaves together, using other ants as sewing needles and thread. These were best left alone. If they were disturbed, intentionally or accidentally, they sought revenge, giving a painful bite and needing to be pulled off as the rest of their tribe attacked you in another area. Black ants on the ground have the same nasty habit. Perhaps the most annoying are tiny, almost invisible ants you would never know were there. Small they might be but they like to bring your attention to the fact they are on your feet or legs by sharp, hot nips. When one finds you, all its friends delight in swarming up your pants legs. While none of the ants are actually dangerous, the bites can make you feel sick for a while and make gardening a little less pleasant.

After I lost my knife, we bought a very sharp local wooden-handled one. This was better suited to stripping the vines off shrubs. I was happily hacking away when I managed to slice my hand, which promptly leaked very red blood, making me feel rather sick.

My yelp of surprise brought Michael and Bandusena to the rescue, who got me into the bathroom, feeling sick and very stupid as they treated the cut and stopped the flow of blood. Was it my age that was making me so careless?

Our only neighbour was some distance from the house but on the road near our gate. The frontage was dolled up to impress. They had some very nice trees and shrubs and lovely orchids. The effect was ruined to our eyes by imitation tree stumps etc., made from concrete. We looked down on it at the start of our 'jungle walk'. The owner appeared not to be there much, but he had staff. An elderly lady was sometimes in the ground, and we would wave to her from our higher level. The thing that was most upsetting was a cage in the ground in which a large unhappy dog was kept. As we walked along the higher part with our dogs running around having a lovely time, the poor dog would bark. How I wished we could have let him out to join us. It was only the one point in the land that we could see this house. Unlike the front, the back was ugly with a cement wall, dividing them from us. We planted things against the wall and in front of them had small pawpaw trees growing from seed. One day the small shrubs and trees that were doing so well blocking the ugly wall had all been cut down, and the ground in front that was one day going to be a pawpaw orchard trampled. For some reason, the wall of their house stopped short of our land by the gate so they had access to our side of it. As all their garden was prim and proper and not very large, they did not wish to sully it by bonfires of rubbish. Rather than put their garbage in a bag and leave outside the gate as we did for the garbage truck to pick up, they preferred to dump it on our side and set fire to it. Cans, etc., did not burn and left an unsightly patch. While the servant had his bonfire, I caught sight of him several times collecting the accra nuts that had fallen to the ground from one of our palms. By right, these should have been Bandusena's who did not chew beetle but would collect them to sell or give to his friends. All this and the destroying of the plants by the wall gave us a good reason to complain. The owner managed to get his complaint in first. Two of our coconut palms he declared dangerous. Growing on land above his house, he said that they might one day fall and damage his roof. Had they fallen, they might well have done so, but they did not look as if they had any intention of doing so. He had contacted our landlady, and the two palms received their death sentence. Men arrived to do the deed; the overseer had good English and was most obliging, telling me he would cut up and remove all the trunk. Not only that, he also agreed to cut some slices of the trunk for me, going so far as to ask how many I wanted. Most of the trunks were duly removed before he disappeared for good, leaving a long trunk right across our walking trail. Needless to say, I never got any slices of the wood.

We complained to our landlady about the actions of our neighbour. I felt she could have easily prevented the servant from trespassing on the land and cutting down trees. We had been told that her family had given him the land along the road to build his house on. We were simply told that people do that sort of thing. "Why?" I asked. "They are ignorant and like to annoy!" We were informed by a friend that the owner was a big man in the government and therefore above the law.

A year later, another palm was taken out, by what we think were government orders. This seemed reasonable, as had it fallen down the bank, it could have caused a nasty accident by falling across the road. To our surprise, they came and removed one that looked to us to be quite safe, while the other, which looked most threatening, was left standing. Not long after, the palm we had thought was dangerous did as expected. The day was calm, with no wind or rain.

Michael and I were sitting on the patio, looking in the direction of the palm when, to our amazement, we watched as the palm very slowly started moving, then crashed down across the road. Michael raced off down to our gate and then back along the road. Bandusena appeared and with the agility of a mountain goat, ran down the bank. I followed the way Michael had gone. In all our minds was the more than awful thought that it could have killed someone or at least taken out a car or a tuk-tuk. Mercifully, our fears were unfounded. The palm lay right across the road, completely blocking it, but the only damage was a couple of broken telegraph poles and all the wires across the road.

Bandusena had taken charge, and it was not too long before he had cut the trunk. With a number of other people, half of the trunk was removed, giving access to one-way traffic. The other half was dealt with in the same way, and traffic once again flowed. At times like these, we admired the way people pulled together. People in their cars either sat and waited patiently or got out and helped. There was no honking of horns. Bandusena had not finished. Back in the house, he pointed to a small red patch on the cloth of a puppet. I was slow on the uptake. He then pointed to the divan, which was full of cloth. I opened it, and he pounced on a piece of red material from which he cut two flags to hang on either side of the damaged area with its broken posts and loose wire.

We presumed that either Bandusena or someone else had alerted the authorities. The first thing the next day, men arrived to replace the broken concrete posts and fix the power lines. We were impressed. We did wonder if we would be held responsible. We were never approached.

Accidents with fallen palms are not uncommon. A coconut from a palm on the roadside, almost opposite us, dropped a nut and killed a baby girl. We knew nothing of this until we saw the palm being cut down and asked why. Strangely, only a few weeks before, men had been picking the coconuts from that palm, tossing them into the road. Traffic obediently stopped and waited until the nuts had been gathered. Sadly, one ready to fall had been missed.

One day Bandusena gave us a King coconut each, having opened the top for us and leaving us to it. After drinking the water, we were keen to get to the jelly. Rather than call Bandusena to split them in half for us, Michael decided he would do it. Placing the coconut on the stone floor was the first mistake. He attacked it with his hatchet; it bounced away like a live animal. Each time he hit it, it flew across the kitchen with Michael in hot pursuit. It looked so funny I rolled up in laughter. Bandusena, hearing the noise, appeared just as Michael finally killed his coconut. The jelly it contained was quite firm and came out and rolled across the now messy floor. Seeing the mess the combat had caused, Bandusena took the other coconut, placed it in one hand, struck it once neatly with the hatchet, handed us the two halves before cleaning up the floor, which by then was covered in bits of fibre and coconut. Disappointed after all that, the kernel was hard not jelly; the dogs had most of it.

I was always surprised to find a fruit or vegetable that I had never seen before. Bandusena gave Michael something he called Larva Loo. Michael called to me, "Come and try something awful." Not a very enticing invitation. I did not find it too awful, just rather strange. The yellow flesh was dry and crumbly, a little like a stale sponge cake. With that in mind, we poured kithul, a syrup made from the nectar of the kithul palm. It then made a pleasant dish. In the centre of the fruit was a large seed, like an elongated conker. Interestingly, it had started growing a root. Planted in a pot, we very soon had a nice little tree which later we put in the ground. We had a friend who claimed he had every fruit tree that grew in Sri Lanka. When asked, he admitted he had not got a Lave Loo. We dug ours up; now it was a nice sapling and added it to his collection.

The way we eat certain fruits very often differs from the way they are eaten in other countries. Unripe, sliced mango is sold from vendors around the bus and train stations. It is salted and sprinkled with chili powder. I love mangoes when ripe and find this treatment of my favourite fruit a little odd. Another favourite of ours is avocado. Here they make it into a drink with sugar. It is okay but rather a waste we feel. They no doubt feel the same about us when we eat our avocado with salt, pepper, onions, and chili.

One product of the coconut we had never tried before was the dry, almost fluffy white ball obtained from a coconut that has just started to grow and then been harvested in its youth.

Not all of the land was fenced. To one side, the lane was widened, and some of the banana plants and trees were taken out. After that, we got some unexpected visitors. Cows wandered in, rather thin cows but surprisingly agile, climbing up a steep bank. They did no damage, and I lived in hope of some dung for the garden. As they never found much food to their liking, they saw no need to deposit us a little gift.

We had a number of fish in the pond and the bathing pool. What I did not expect to find was a dead fish on the mat where Lucy puts all her toys. It only had a small piece eaten out of it. Later, I found a five-inch fish of the same type floating in the pond. The same evening, we spotted Lucy with something in her mouth; she placed it on the grass. The same fish! None of the dogs care very much for the pond, and when a fish swims by, they draw back. On occasions, we had seen the two young civets near the pond and wondered if they go fishing at night.

Palm squirrels are common and can be seen all the time. They are interesting little chaps that scold a lot for no apparent reason. On the patio, we had some hanging baskets lined with coconut fiber.

One very industrious little squirrel pulled vast quantities of the fibre out of a basket. He managed to carry a large quantity by stuffing it in his mouth, so he looked as if he had a beard. He then headed for a Moroccan lamp hanging from the rafters. Running along the rafters and down the chain the lamp hung on, he quickly stuffed the fibre in the lamp. This continued until the lamp was completely full. We were never sure if it raised a family in the lamp. Months later, the squirrel or its look-alike took all the fibre in the lamp out and carried it off to the roof.

We spent the first six months without ever seeing any monkeys enjoying our land. Then a troop finally decided we were quite friendly, and seven of them could mostly be seen on our roof or in the trees, helping themselves to the fruit when it was still green. They were never bold enough to come up to us to take any proffered fruit. They soon got the hang of how things lay, and when the dogs would dash around barking at them, they would sit above in a tree tossing down half-eaten fruit or a small branch. They did not come to the ground and knew the dogs could not reach them. One very bold male was very nearly caught. We were sitting eating lunch on the patio when the dogs, barking and rushing up with the monkey ahead of them, dashed through the patio, knocking over a chair in its hurry, and across the grass and up a palm. The dogs had no chance. They treated us much the same way as they did the dogs.

They would glance at us as they pulled off a sour sop or some fruit and then dash up to the roof to eat it, or part of it. The uneaten part they would toss back to us.

Little delights often happened in the garden quite unexpectedly. While digging in the garden, I came across a small lizard egg. I carried it into the house in the hope that we could see it hatch. It forestalled me, hatching in my hand, jumping down and shooting off as if it knew just exactly where it was going.

Chapter Twenty Five

The Well

Our water came from a well, a very modern, civilised well. No winding up a long rope with a bucket on the end. A pump resided in the pump house, near the well and tank, and when switched on, would obligingly pump the water up to a large tank which had pipes leading to the bathrooms, kitchen, and all outside taps. The switch for the pump was just outside the kitchen.

Simple for us to turn on when the taps ran dry but rather harder for either of us to remember to turn off before it overflowed. Michael decided we needed a time switch. When we left the UK, we had only taken a small amount of our tools with us. It seemed unlikely that such a thing as a time switch would be among the bits in the tool box. Feeling it was worth a try, Michael looked and amazingly found one. He soon had it fixed up and announced our troubles were over; it would turn itself on for a set period each morning and then turn off. No more dry taps or tank overflowing.

Next morning, I heard him shouting, "Someone has turned the pump off." As it is too high for the dogs to reach, it was clear that either I or Bandusena was the guilty party. I truthfully claimed not to have touched it. Bandusena had caught the drift of the outburst and pointed out the water overflowing from the tank, down the bank, creating a rather attractive waterfall.

After studying the plug, Michael explained to both Bandusena and me how it worked if left alone. I rather think Bandusena knew how it should work, and for my part, I knew I must not touch it, which I had no desire to do anyway.

Michael and I now settled down to breakfast. Bandusena came up to us and drew our attention to the fact that once again we had a mini waterfall. Finally, the timer cooperated and we had no more waterfalls or dry taps.

The water in our well was a very long way down, and we did wonder if it ever ran dry and what we would do if it did. On enquiring, we learned that wells and tanks benefited if they were cleaned regularly. We got Bandusena to arrange for someone to come and do the cleaning. Rather stupidly, I expected a professional well-cleaning outfit to turn up in a van. Instead, two young men arrived in a Tuk-tuk, with ropes, a pump, and a large, long hose. We gathered round to watch. The pump with the hose attached was lowered down into the well. A cable was plugged into the electric and water flowed out through the large borehole of the hose. We soon had a river running through the undergrowth. Rather wasteful but the hose was far too heavy to direct it towards shrubs that would have benefited from a good dousing. There was far more water in the well than we had thought. Finally, it was more or less empty. We could see rocks, bricks, and sludge at the bottom. The younger of the two men was very well dressed in white denim shorts and a red 'T' shirt, both of which looked new. He was the one to go down the well, doing so without stripping off. A rope was put down the end of the well until it reached the bottom. The other man and Bandusena hung on to the top of the rope. The young man hung on the rope with his hands and walked down the side of the well, trusting his life that the other two would not let go. Earlier, Bandusena had got two of our buckets; these now were lowered down empty and pulled up full of all the muck at the bottom. Considering the amount that came up, it was surprising that it had not blocked the well from filling. When all the sludge etc. had been removed, the man in the red shirt came up slowly, weeding the sides of the well as he came. He was a little wet and splattered but in the main quite clean. Already, the well was filling up.

Meanwhile, Bandusena had turned on all the taps, emptying the tank. We then had to find sponges that they asked for. Workmen, however skilled, rarely bring their own tools. The long, extending ladder we had failed to find a buyer for in England was now hauled up the bank and put against the tank, into which both men disappeared. The whole entertainment lasted two and a half hours and cost us the equivalent of £24.

Cleaning the Well

Chapter Twenty Six

Domestic Jobs

The house we rented was in perfect condition, but we had pictures we wished to hang on the walls. There were quite a number of paintings and drawings friends had done, and some of my own efforts. We had not thought to bring picture hooks with us and found none in the shops. Just as well, when Bandusena saw that we were about to ruin the walls so perfect, he phoned our landlady. She asked us not to put things on the wall but to hang them from a picture rail that ran high along the walls. At that point in the conversation, Bandusena appeared like a genie with a bag full of brass hooks that go over the picture rail. This would be fine, but the ceiling was very high so all the pictures would have to hang from cords a couple of meters long. A search among my sewing items unearthed what appeared to be a limitless amount of black cord. Our ladder was brought in, and Michael climbed up with a picture, a long length of cord attached to one ring at the back of the picture, passed it over the hook, and unrolled the cord until Bandusena and I below judged it to be the perfect height. He descended holding the place on the cord and attached it to the other ring, back up and hung it on the hook. Simple except we had about 30 pictures of varied sizes and also a set of six to group together.

A few of the smaller ones, we put in the bedrooms and used blue tack to hold them to the wall. All the pictures found their place over a number of days. More cord had been bought, pictures moved along, adjusted, and adjusted again.

We had several Moroccan lamps. A large one would have looked splendid in the centre of the ceiling over the living area. In the place we wished to hang it, hung a modern lamp with large steel rings surrounding it, later to be used by a magpie robin. With no step ladder and no place to prop a ladder, it was a puzzle how it got there and how we could remove and replace it with our own lamp. The problem was easily solved. Our landlady asked us not to remove it.

Eventually, we got all our lamps up, but it entailed a lot of work. First, one of the large kitchen tables was dragged under the lamp to be replaced, then another was placed on top of it. Michael is six foot, but he still could not reach, so a smaller coffee table was added. To get up on this contraption, a bit of mountain climbing had to be done. Since both the kitchen tables were the same size, another table had to be put next to them to enable him to climb up. He was then able to reach the existing light and shade, remove it, and fit our own. At one point, in reaching down for the lamp, the top table wobbled frighteningly. Bandusena and I grabbed the table legs, and all was well. Over a period of several days, five lamps were changed in this manner without accident. Our ladder was becoming quite indispensable.

The ladder came into play again when we found that we had a pretty little rat making regular visits to our kitchen. We had seen it peeping down at us from between the wall and ceiling where it had made a hole. I saw no point in blocking the hole when the same rat could so easily vacate the roof into the yard and come in through the windows or doors. Michael and Bandusena did not agree and set about blocking every hole they could see. Bandusena, having blocked the latest hole, had left for his lunch. Michael surveyed his work and spotted another small hole.

I was in the house when I heard a crash and the sound of broken glass. Rushing out to the kitchen, I saw Michael sprawled on the floor with the ladder and a bits of broken glass. Alone without anyone holding the ladder, he had decided to prop it against a cabinet and get to the hole. The ladder, as ladders are prone to do, slipped and down he crashed. The door of the cabinet had flown open, and a number of drinking glasses flew out. Michael appeared uncut but looked as white as a sheet. I tried to help him up, but he did not seem able to move until he had rested for a bit. I phoned Garmeni, our Tuk-tuk driver, as he had some English, and he in turn phoned Bandusena. By the time they arrived, Michael had got up and put himself under the shower. As the glass was swept up and the ladder removed, the two of them managed to make it clear that it was Bandusena's job to do things and old people should not climb ladders unsupervised.

We were often a worry and bewilderment to them over some of the things we did. We had a tent lying unused, and we got it out to air. The sight of it brought back happy memories and a wish to go camping again. Michael decided to erect it near where we had the hammock and spend the night in it. There, above the house, all would be silent, and if he did not put the outer cover on, he could look up at the stars. A wonderful idea. I thought if I could get Lucy to join me, I would sleep in it the following night. The idea was not a good one. What appeared to be a flat surface had a definite slope. The area was large but not so between the coconut palm, which might just decide to drop a nut on the tent. He spent a far from enjoyable night, and when it started to rain, he gave up.

Often other people had cause to wonder at our antics. We both laughed when Michael returned from cycling into Galle to buy a pair of shorts. Sizes vary, and often what is on the label has no relation to the actual size. He had gone into the changing room to try them on. Returning home, he discovered he no longer had the key to lock his bike, just the fob. He then remembered hearing a crunch as he was changing and now felt sure it had fallen from his pocket onto the changing room floor. Turning round, he cycled back to the shop. On arrival, he found the staff had changed. "Perhaps you went to the wrong shop," I butted in. "No, I know it was the same one, different staff." Without trying to explain or looking at the merchandise, he went straight into the changing room. Not seeing the key, he went down on his hands and knees and swept the floor with his hand. No key. As he got up, he saw the staff were watching him through the open door. He nodded to them, smiled, and left. They all just stood looking very bewildered.

We often lost count of the days; they passed so quickly. We had arranged to give a small tea party to a couple of families on Sunday. It was also the same day the coconut pickers had been told to come. The day dawned with us unaware it was the agreed Sunday. I moved a chair in the kitchen and a bit fell off for no apparent reason. Almost immediately Bandusena moved a coffee table to sweep, and a clay Inca head I'd left on it rolled off, splitting in three. We hardly had time to pick up the bits when Michael knocked the knob off a dining room chair.

Remembering that such accidents come in threes, we felt sure the rest of the day would go smoothly, "Coconuts," Announces Bandusena. "Tomorrow," I reply. Bandusena knows tomorrow and the days of the week. Bandusena, "Today is Sunday." Me, "Tomorrow is Sunday." Michael refused to take sides.

All three of us consult the "Born Free" calendar. The dates are shown in small print; none of us have our glasses. We move on to the Orangutan calendar. I point out I have crossed off Friday. To my way of thinking, it proves the day is Saturday. Bandusena still does not agree, insisting it is Sunday. Michael keeps quiet, not knowing who is correct. I turn on the computer and Michel finds his watch.

We put on our specs. Bandusena is correct; it is Sunday. He also is now conveying that someone or something is happening on Monday. We thought we would go into that later. We now have to prepare for our tea party. It is still only morning, but we have nothing in the house to give them. Michael starts calling me. "Where is the tea? Bandusena needs to make tea for the coconut pickers." I know he knows where the tea is kept. I go into the kitchen. The tea caddy is on the table. I look inside. What was I seeing? I could not believe it. The tea that was always there was now replaced by fine black stuff looking like soil and certainly not tea. A year before, Sita had given me a large pack of tea to take back to England. We used some for tea-drinking friends and even gave some away, but then we had moved to Sri Lanka and the tea had come back with us. It must have gone past its sell-by date, died, and turned to dust. Rather fortunate for us that it was discovered before I attempted to serve it to our guests.

Michael went off on his bike for cake, cookies, fruit, and ice cream and of course, tea. He remembered it all but forgot the tea. We also decided we might need more ice cream as even the adults eat it. Bandusena said he would go, but Michael felt two items were easy to remember and came back with it all. The coconut pickers arrived. Tea was made and all was under control. At eleven thirty, the phone rang. One of the families was asking if we were ready for them. I gasped and heard him say something about a daughter having evening classes. The line went dead. He phoned again, and again the line went dead. I was left with no idea when to expect them. About to phone them back, the phone rang. It was Sita to tell us Shiromi will take a certain number of coconuts. I finally got back to the friend who had phoned, and it was agreed to keep to the original time of four or four thirty. When I went to tell Michael, I found he was chopping up fruit to make a salad, thinking we were about to receive our guest. Finding the fruit was not good quality, he smothered it in Kithul and put it in the fridge.

The coconuts had been picked and counted, and we managed to scrape up the correct payment before they left. We did wonder if anyone would actually turn up, but faithful Manny phoned to reassure us he was on his way. Manny and his family arrived, not in his famous old rattletrap; the spring had gone, and we rather thought that had happened a long time ago, but now the brakes also had given up. They turned up in a borrowed Tuk-tuk. Manny driving, his wife, two large sons, and his daughter squeezed into the two passenger seats. LJS's friend arrived with his wife and daughter; from then on everything went well as far as we were concerned. Food was eaten and Manny's son who I taught how to cane chair seats and was familiar with the place did all the washing up. He then entertained the girls by showing them a rubber snake we kept on the patio. The two girls had been a little shy at first but were now both giggling and feigning horror.

Lucy was a bit taken aback with all this strange goings-on, but when Bandusena put the remaining biscuits and ice cream in the dog bowls, all three dogs decided the day had turned out well. It was Michael's 71st birthday the following day, and Manny had given him a very nice sarong. Bandusena had taken the opportunity to talk to Manny, asking him to make sure we remembered that our landlady was visiting the following day.

We were very lucky with our landlady; we got on well both with her and various other members of the family who would visit on occasions. This time she arrived with her sister-in-law, the same age as myself but an animated and tiny little lady. She had been brought up in the house and so regarded it, as is the custom here, as her ancestral home. To us, this sounded very grand, but nearly all the houses we had looked at to rent were ancestral homes. All were less than a hundred years old. Now we were asked if we would mind forty old-aged pensioners visiting us when they had a day's outing. This sounded rather fun, but I pointed out we could not serve tea to such a large number; we only had two cups and saucers. This was fine; they would take tea before they arrived and just take a tour of the house.

When the day arrived, a large coach drove up the drive. All the pensioners were female. As they alighted, we played the part of lord and lady of the Manor, welcoming each one, some with handshakes and others bowing with our hands together as in prayer, taking our cue from how each one greeted us. They all made the rounds of each room. None saw more of the garden other than stepping out of the coach and a few steps to the house. We were then told to stand together and had our photo taken, and I was presented with a tea cosy they had made. As they left, we again shook hands or bowed to each in turn. The coach miraculously managed to back down the steep drive perfectly. Then we saw Bandusena dashing after it, brandishing a pair of sandals one lady had left behind. Later, we found another pair on the patio.

By the end of the first year, the whole place was the dream I had visualised. The dogs, Rosie and Blackie, had adopted us, and little Lucy Loo was my constant companion; we doted on each other. One snag: I could not leave the place, not even for a short trip to the shops, without her crying. The other two would accompany me, being used to all the traffic. Lucy would go no further than our gate.

Our landlady and lawyer visited at the end of our year, and we paid and signed for another year. All was fine until LJS drove up the drive and joined us. He had entered our life again some months after we got our shipment. He had come three times with foreigners he had managed to pick up who were looking for a house to buy. He then just about ignored them and told us things like we must renew our insurance, etc. It was much the same as when he had taken us to the German lady's house, for no apparent reason. The couples were always very nice and apologetic as they too must have felt as we did when with the German lady. I then banned him from the house, and we saw him no more. Now he turns up, telling us the gate was open. I was very upset and thought it strange and wrong that our nice landlady had invited him. She told me she had not, but he knew the date our agreement ran out and had come to make sure we signed for another year so he could pocket his commission each month.

As it turned out, we were not bothered by LJS again. We had another worry; the family had sold some land on the other side of the lane that runs along the side of the land. It had been bought by builders who set about making the lane much wider, and in doing so, taking a small part of what had been our land. Worse was to come. They set up a loudspeaker at the entrance of the widened lane and music if it can be called that¾blared out by which they hoped to attract passing cars on the road to interest them in purchasing, yet to be built one of the 40 new homes, handing out leaflets, most of which blew away in the wind. Our worry was that we would now have another road near us and more traffic if forty houses were to be built. Fortunately, the whole project petered out. Instead, the main road that was always noisy became worse as huge machines arrived and started to widen it. We were at first told that some of the land bordering the road would be taken which would entail the removal of many trees including a beautiful and productive jak tree and also our gate posts. If that was done then the gate for next door and all their wall would also have to go right up to their house and much of their garden. Had our neighbour been a nobody this no doubt would have taken place. However, the owner of next door was some bigwig in government we were told. Plans were suddenly modified. We still lost some trees but not as many and our gate post was saved along with all of the neighbours. Instead, the shop and house the other side of the road further down had their walls rebuilt right up to the house. We felt sad for them and could not see how making the road just a little wider would help in any way. Our jak tree was left but now right on the edge and it was deemed dangerous and sentenced to death. That took many months to get the permit allowing it to be felled. The widening of the road adjacent to our land took over a year. On occasions, we were unable to get in or out of our gate, a deep gully having been dug between us and the road. With the clearing of so many trees on both sides of the road, we now could not only see the road but also the highway that ran parallel to it. Traffic still used the road but while work was in progress often only one lane, which resulted in more horn blowing to add to the noise of the huge machines tipping gravel, etc. Our paradise was being eroded before our eyes.

Sadly, we informed our landlady that we would not be signing for a third year. We had loved the place. If only we could have lifted it up and placed it in some unspoilt area, it would have been heaven. Such miracles can only be a dream. We would have to move.

Chapter Twenty Seven

A Van for the Dogs

Until we made the decision to move, we had lived happily without any transport, apart from Michael's fold-up bike. We could phone the Tuk-tuk for short runs or emergencies, or catch a bus into Galle. Neither of these would be an option when moving with the dogs. Unlike many countries where buses carry livestock as well as humans, we had never seen a non-human passenger on the buses in Sri Lanka.

We were still in touch with Sunil, the tuk-tuk driver who had once worked for my late husband and me in Galle many years before. Sunil put us in touch with Asitha, who dealt in vans, selling or renting them. We rented one of his vans.

Sri Lankan dogs do not, as a rule, ride in cars or vans, and our dogs were well aware of this. Vehicles were to be dodged on the road or chased down our drive.

Asitha had been very obliging and removed the back seat of the van we rented. We had arranged to have a coconut mat made to fit in the space at the back. Coconut door mats were appreciated by all the dogs. Lucy had completely destroyed one mat as a puppy. All of them liked rolling on the replacement. We hoped adding the mat would be an inducement for them to enjoy the van.

We left the van at the top of the drive and showed it to them and the nice mat at the back. We left the back open so they could explore it. They showed no interest beyond sniffing at the wheels. After a few days, it was clear a little encouragement had to be used. Rosie, being the oldest and smallest, is easy to pick up and would be the first to do a test run. Michael picked her up, putting her on the mat at the back with a doggy treat next to her. She was not to be bribed. Ignoring both the treat and the nice new mat, she moved to the seats in the centre of the van. I sat down next to her. Michael started the engine, and we moved off. Rosie was not a happy dog. We drove to the nearest beach, parked, and got out, expecting Rosie to follow. She did not move. Again, Michael picked her up and walked down the beach with her. The beach we had chosen was people-free, and she was put down facing the sea. She was determined not to take part in our silly game and turned around to have her back to that big expanse of water. We jumped up and down and ran short distances like a couple of loonies. Rosie sat as if made of stone. Michael crossed the river that divided the beach. No response from Rosie. He walked out of sight, no response from Rosie. I moved off watching her; she did not care. We gave up. Michael picked her up, and we got back in the van. Rosie had not enjoyed her first ride as we had hoped. Perhaps she thought we were going to the vet as the only time she had been in a car and a tuk-tuk was when she had treatment at the vet.

Next day, we put Lucy in the van. She also rejected the mat and chose to sit next to me in the middle seats. She got half on my lap, trembling like a leaf all the short distance. When lifted out of the van and put down, she jumped back in, looking at me and whimpering. I had to assure her we had no intention of abandoning her. Again, we gave up and came home.

Blackie never got her turn. She had witnessed the other two being put in and made sure she was around when we wanted to take her. The next outing, we took both Lucy and Rosie. I sat with them both, Lucy no longer trembling and Rosie taking an interest in looking out the window. We let them out on some scrubland above the beach, and they started to explore. Lucy looked back every few steps to make sure I was following. From then on, outings to the beaches with the two became fun. On returning home, Blackie would sniff them. Later, she would watch as Lucy and Rosie jumped in the van willingly as soon as we did.

We could tell she was interested, but she still refused to jump in. One day, Michael picked her up and put her in. This must have been what she was waiting for. We went to Galle Fort and up on the Ramparts. Not being sure what Blackie would do, we put a collar and lead on her. We soon dropped the lead, and all three of them rushed off with Blackie in the lead, having a wonderful time. From then on, we could never go out in the van without all three making sure they came too.

Before we left the UK, many friends had said they would come and visit. We looked forward to showing friends and relations all the wonders of Sri Lanka. For one reason or another, no one came, until just before moving, when Michael's lifelong friend Garth and his wife Marieta came and stayed for two weeks. We really enjoyed their visit and wished more of our friends had come. By then, we had decided where to move and took them to see our future home.

We kept visiting the new place months before moving in, doing the garden and getting the dogs used to the place. Even before we actually moved, I was having second thoughts. We still miss our dream home. Road works continued, and finally, the death warrant on the jak tree came about. As I write, the road works have passed the house. We have visited our old home, a mistake. The garden is now overgrown again as nature takes over, and the trails likewise. Even the dogs found it hard to follow what used to be our "Jungle jaunts". The seat Bandusena had put up by the cashew tree has succumbed to the wood ants.

Our first year has been as near to paradise as anyone could hope to get. Progress, in the widening of the road, had spoiled the second year, though in hindsight perhaps we should have stuck it out. Our good friend Manny passed away. He had leukaemia and had not expected to live to an old age, even going to India to seek health through meditation and plan the future for his family after he was gone. One day when visiting us, we had told him our decision to move. He said he would help us find a place. Two days later, we were shocked to learn he had died after being knocked off his motorbike just a few yards from his home,

Life will always have its ups and downs, to make us grateful for all the wonderful parts.

We did move further south and had two lovely ponds built. The two acres are less interesting than our former home but with a magnificent mango tree covered in orchids and air plants that rains mangos down on us for about a month each year. Some have been partly eaten by birds, bats, squirrels, and monkeys; however, there are still hundreds left for us and friends to enjoy. We also have other fruits including rambutan; unlike the one in our former home, here we are able to enjoy the fruits, it being a more down-to-earth size.

The dogs enjoy the place and do not appear to be homesick for their former home. In one part of the ground that is meant to be a tea plantation, there is a large area of fine black soil. We were told that the area was used to refine salt once, and the black is the charcoal. The dogs love it; it is their favourite place. All three, plus a male dog left with us by the landlord, dig like mad, making deep holes in the fine black soil to lie in. The ground is not even, so you can look up and see just four heads above ground.

Riding in the van is part of our girls' life. Lucy will not go if I don't. For the most part, we all go out together. We now have bought our own 26-year-old rust bucket Nissan van. Local people often suggest we buy a new car. We and our dogs much prefer the old van. The dogs feel superior sitting in the van, taking it in turns to sit up front, and now and then all three try to take a hand, or paw, in driving. When Blackie is up front, she feels the urge to give us both big sloppy wet kisses, perhaps because for once our heads are more or less level with hers. People still react when seeing them in the van, as if they have never seen a dog before. Some ask where the dogs come from, thinking they must be some special breed. Women and children behave normally and just look happy to see the dogs. Men point and shout "Dogs" at us just in case we have not noticed three are in the van with us. Others bark or make strange noises. Our three either ignore such rude manners or jump up and bark, which makes them move off.

The highlight of the year in our new home was a visit from our sister, Jennie, and my goddaughter, Claire. Having them stay with us made the place suddenly feel like home. My only wish was that they could have been with us in our Dream Home.

Bandusena visits us two or three times a month to cut the grass and do any other jobs. All the dogs are always overjoyed to see him.

Amazingly, we learn that our former home remains empty. I start wishing we were still there, remembering all the happy times. We decided we can't go back and start all over again restoring the land as we did before, as nature had taken over as soon as we left. Our time in this world must be running out, and we need to seek new challenges that are not so physically demanding.

Our life is made easier by having a delightful young lady, Nalika, spend her morning with us, cleaning and cooking. She has become part of our household. The dogs love her, and she loves them. We are considerably further from Galle but still managed to visit our dear friends, Sita, and her family in the Fort most weeks.

One day, we may move again, if we find another Shina Niwasa.

(Dream Home).

END